Get a Life

Setting Your LifeCompass for Success

Nicholas Bate

MJF BOOKS
NEW YORK

Published by MJF Books
Fine Communications
322 Eighth Avenue
New York, NY 10001

Get a Life
Library of Congress Control Number 2006922811
ISBN-13: 978-1-56731-784-8
ISBN-10: 1-56731-784-7

This edition published by MJF Books in arrangement with Capstone Publishing Limited, a Wiley Company.

Printed in the United States of America.

VB 10 9 8 7 6 5 4 3 2 1

Contents

Thanks

To Anne for her incredible love, belief and support.

To Jessica for her love, support of the underdog, her tenacity and perceptual paradoxes; Jacob for his love, philosophy, rowing and unfailing appreciation of my cooking; Isaac for his love, humour, air-guitar playing and companionship; Mum for her belief, example and support; Dad for his energy, example and support.

Also to Richard Burton for the initial break and John Moseley for his continued support in challenging times.

Chapter 1
Get a Life?

Get a life!

The desire to get a life, to restore work/life balance, to 'come alive' (but without the aid of Pepsi) has never been stronger.

Our lives are pressured: it appears that while anybody and everyone can communicate with us at all times, we rarely have the time to communicate with ourselves or our loved ones. Our lives often appear to be one-dimensional: work, and only work, be that managing the household or managing the team. It's not, of course, that ours is the first generation to be under pressure, but maybe we truly are the first generation where the pressure is all-pervading, where our coping strategies have reached their natural limits and the ability to think has become the slowest process in the melée of our busy lives. A process which competes poorly against the likes of the internet, globalization, dual-parent working. We are on the critical path. The pressure is thus relentless: even if we are not working 24/7, we certainly think we are. Constant fatigue is kept at bay through the drip-feeding of caffeine, anxiety and fear-induced adrenalin.

Yet deep down we each know that we have more potential: there's so much more we want to do and be. We have dreams and visions which unfortunately all too often seem to be dependent upon winning the lottery. Perhaps more frustratingly, there seems to be little way out of the chaos of everyday life and no simple way of stepping up to the life we would really like to live. It's all too easy to lose sight, in the apparent chaos of downsized/rightsized organizations, growing families and work/life balance uncertainties, of what we really want.

That is the reality of life for many people that I meet in my workshops. Certainly there are many, many high points, but too much is only 'OK' and some of it, frankly, is just 'grim'. Of course, compared to the lives of many on this planet these people know, deep down, that their existence is not that bad: compared to some, it is downright fantastic. But unfortunately for them it doesn't feel that good, in fact it forever feels as if a much better way of running their life is 'so close' but out of reach.

There is a way out

There is a way out, though, and it is straightforward. It doesn't require you to escape to Tuscany, give it all up and retire to Wales, downsize/rightsize (unless you feel those options really will help, of course) or do anything at all complicated. The way out is simply to adjust your way of thinking and act in some very specific ways that you can customize to fit your own situation, and then to follow them through with some reflection and straightforward actions. For many of us, the biggest challenge of the situation in which we find ourselves is the lost ability to use our 'reflective' intelligence: that powerful thought process which allows us to resolve many of the challenges in our lives. But before we explore this approach, let's be clear on a few of the tempting methods that do not work. You may be using one of them at the moment and, as it's not working, it's always nice to know that it's not just you and that now would be a good time to ditch that particular approach.

Crazy, no-return, doomed-to-failure strategies

There are plenty of these. We've all tried them (me too, of course). I encounter people using them on my workshops; they are usually mentioned when I'm coaching and I often find that new corporate clients have them embedded into their infrastructure.

But the truth is that they simply don't work. I've seen some people try and use them for years; it's not about lack of persistence with any of these. They are the wrong strategies in the first place.

False strategy number 1: 'It's just a stage in my life'

(The one where we tell ourselves 'it's just a phase and it'll get easier'.)

Well, it's true – of course – that we do have different stages in our lives such as the lots-of-exams stage, the house-full-of-toddlers stage, promotion-on-the-horizon stage, house-purchase stage, just-going-through-a-sticky-patch stage, etc. So perhaps the best thing for you is just to hang on and it will sort itself out … Possibly: a bit of that is fine. But think about it, reflect back over your life to date. Things don't necessarily seem to be getting any easier, do they? Once you have completed one stage another is on the way. Call it entropy, call it chaos: your life – or perhaps more strictly, the environment around your life – is just becoming more demanding. Now is the time to start managing it a little better. And that is the most important indicator that this strategy of 'just go with the flow, it'll work itself through' is not an ideal one. You know when it's working and you certainly know when it's not.

In fact, apart possibly from retirement – when for many perhaps too much grinds to a halt – there are no naturally easy stages; every stage has its particular challenges. That's the elegance of the approach we are going to look at: it is customizable to you, the situation and your particular challenge. You have to make them easy: I'm going to show you how.

False strategy number 2: 'I simply need to get more efficient'

(The one where you simply feel there's a magic technique which you are missing and you only need to discover it for everything to improve.)

A dangerous and commonly employed strategy: this is the 'I simply need to work longer and/or harder and that will sort the problem' strategy. This does at least have some historical precedence. There was a time – both historically and for some of us, particularly if we are over thirty, in our own individual careers – when our days were not so loaded and when, therefore, there was some capacity for upping the workload. Consequently, an initial response to the challenges we are discussing was better time management (you'll have noticed that there is always a new book or new system available on time management) or working harder (getting up half an hour earlier – that's two and a half hours per week just for doing email) or outsourcing (ironing, children, fun). But thresholds are soon met. There is simply a limit to how much stuff anyone can do, even to how much we can outsource. Can you really cope with three inter-scheduled nannies? (No, honestly – this was cited to me on a recent workshop.)

At the same time too much efficiency, too much working and too much outsourcing all cause their own problems. Too much efficiency means no slack or downtime. Slack is part of the process of being human: it allows us to use our reflective intelligence, to just think 'how am I doing?' and enjoy life. Too much working means that we are not playing. Play is a particularly human attribute: it energizes us and allows us to remain authentic. Too much outsourcing means that we lose touch with what is happening: ironically, we often lose touch with those very people that outsourcing was meant to help. Many people are at their efficiency threshold and many hit it a long time ago. Remember there was a time when the rate of delivery of post to the in-tray was a limiting factor? Now, in an 'instant' world, we are the slowest factor around.

False strategy number 3: Escapism

(This is the one where we employ rationalization and defensiveness, and are simply not honest with ourselves.)

This is perhaps the most worrying false strategy: simply believing that something is not happening. Drown the pain. Watch more TV, drink more. Change your job. Blame others: the boss, your partner. Enough said. Not a great strategy and certainly one which only leads to more chaos in life. Be very careful about adopting a 'victim' mentality, about blaming others. That is not to say that we should let a poorly run organization or a bullying manager off the hook. But, whatever the problem, the first step is to take responsibility for our own life, to decide: victim or volunteer?

A way out of this chaos

Yes, well, stuff happens. And it's history. Learn and move on.

There really is a way out: to set your 'personal compass' or LifeCompass. This alternative response, and the one with which we are concerned, is to examine our lives a little more closely. To reconsider (or consider for the first time) what we really want. And how we are working. Nothing heavy, all very straightforward. But, despite that, to make some fundamental shifts, perhaps break some limiting patterns, such as some ways of working which currently hinder us. Some examples might be:

- *Creating an integrated life. Instead of fighting the individual components – work, family, money – bring them together so that they support each other. They need not be at odds with each other. Simply imagine how much time would be saved if each aspect of your life supported the others, as opposed to being in conflict with them.*
- *Creating some true motivators beyond money, pressure, adrenalin and caffeine. Hey, money is a great motivator – but usually for what people believe it can do for them or get them, things like freedom, fun, love. How about if you went straight for what you really wanted? I'll look at the fast-track approach to such desires later.*
- *Regularly investing in ourselves. I know, it does seem a little odd. But think about it. You are organic and fragile. You're working long hours, your diet is not as good as it should be and you're getting too little appreciation. Crikey, no wonder you are on a low par.*
- *Realizing how much mindset dictates results. It's OK. I did promise that it wouldn't be heavy. But how about if you found a very fast way to get even*

better results, and how about if this was easy to do?

- *An ongoing approach. One which allowed you to keep on track for the life you wanted, whatever changes might come your way.*
- *And of course, happiness and contentment. You'll no doubt have realized by now that many of the generators of happiness – such as more money, chocolate, a great film or book, conversation, sex or a holiday, whilst all being great fun and certainly not being underrated, tend not to last until the next event. And even some of those can have diminishing returns (there are only so many films we want to see in a day) or reverse effects (too much chocolate …). The one proven reliable source of happiness is living a life which both realizes and releases your talents. And that is what the LifeCompass is about.*

That, and a whole lot more, is exactly what we are going to be achieving in the rest of this book.

A life unexamined … is a life not fully lived.
The Dalai Lama

Chapter 2
The LifeCompass

Let's back-up for a moment and put this in context to help you to an even better understanding. Way back in 1988, when I started the personal development consultancy I run, Strategic Edge, a compass was a natural choice for our logo. We were after all about supporting the development of individuals, helping them 'find their way', helping them realize and release their potential.

Now, a decade and a half later, our logo has metamorphosed but its message is the same, as is our purpose: we all have enormous potential and increasingly each and every one of us wants to get at it. Many of us have already started and want to accelerate and build momentum. Whatever your current stage of work on your personal plans, wherever you are with your career and personal development, this book will help you to be successful, however you might define that ubiquitous word.

In all my experience of teaching those people whose goal is to do more and to be more, whatever their position or background, I've discovered that the real breakthrough comes when they understand their personal compass or LifeCompass. This is a concept which we have developed at Strategic Edge over our fifteen years of research and teaching to help individuals decide, firstly, what is important to them and, secondly, how to achieve it. The keys are decision and action. Decision on its own is not enough. Action completes the change. But action without clarity can be futile.

Never has this kind of thinking, reflection and action been more important. As our way of life becomes increasingly more complex, we find it increasingly difficult as individuals to reserve our own time and the space we need to restore simplicity to our quest. This book will give clear indications on how to do that: to get simplicity without being simplistic, to get depth without jargon and above all to get results which are pragmatic, sustainable and compatible with you, with both your personality (quiet, loud, intellectual, practical …) and your lifestyle (on a strict budget, made it all?). The LifeCompass will allow you to get success with balance and be authentic.

Authenticity

Authenticity? What does that mean? Being who you truly are. Allowing yourself to live to your full potential. To remove the blockers. To grow. To live with passion, to have fun, to contribute, to make a difference: that's being authentic.

The Strategic Edge LifeCompass

Few of us would deliberately set out into uncharted territory without a compass, be it a traditional 'boy scout' dial compass or a more sophisticated GPS device. At worst we'd get lost and never achieve what we had set out to do, but equally we might take an unnecessarily long time to get there – and with no one to blame but ourselves.

That's the challenge for life. There's clearly so much opportunity out there: fascinating, interesting and rewarding work; perfect health; fantastic relationships; financial independence; a world to explore; people to help; amazing children to support to adulthood; new ways to cook; learning to unicycle … but how do we get to it? Some people seem to get there but then lose it ('… she has an amazing job but has become ill because of stress'). Some seem to get there but at an inappropriate cost ('… he's the MD of a prestigious company, but never saw his children while they were growing up'). Some never even get near ('I'd love to do something in design, but …'). And where is 'there' anyway ('… I'm a multimillionaire. I thought I'd got there. But I'm not happy.')? And what's 'it'? Different things for different people, certainly. By the way, it's not that we can't gain a lot from getting lost sometimes, I know I have; we'll find some fascinating inspiration along the way. It's just nice to know that we are lost, so that we can get back on (perhaps a new?) track. We need a compass for our lives. That's what I mean by LifeCompass.

For those of you have read my previous book *Being the Best: the A to Z of Personal Success*, this one is an in-depth analysis of C: compass. If you haven't read *Being the Best* already, you may well find doing so helpful for looking at other characteristics which will support the implementation of your compass strategy. But start here. Everyone needs a LifeCompass. For real people with real relationships, real families and real challenges in real jobs, LifeCompass is a practical strategy.

In this book I want to help you:

- *Decide 'what do I truly want?' and 'what is success for me?' Because despite powerful messages from much of society you'll now be at the point where you have realized that success is not simply money and/or consumer goods, and/or power, and need include none of those. So many people spend a lot of time being unhappy because they haven't got the amount of stuff and the level of wealth that they want. And a smaller but significant group are unhappy because they have all of that but it doesn't give them what they now realize they seek. What's up? Are human beings just perverse? Is it that whatever we don't have, we want? Perhaps, a little. Certainly it is true that we rarely stop and think about what we truly want.*
- *Create straightforward, reliable methods (or strategies) for ensuring that success happens for you; in particular, the use of the LifeCompass. Success is not something which only happens to other people. Luck, good fortune, great ideas are available to all of us.*

- *Step beyond some of the purely simplistic ideas of success.*
- *Realize that success will require work on your part but that it is absolutely, undoubtedly, accessible, and you're probably putting in a lot of work at the moment. Realize that it takes work to be having a bad time all the time. It takes work to be depressed. It takes a lot of energy to work in an unsupportive organization or relationship. How about if you put all this energy into another context to get the life which you really want? You can.*

Time and time again individuals show just what is possible. And time and time again simple observation shows that this can be achieved independently of genes, education qualifications, money, family background and intelligence. Genes, education, qualifications, money, background, intelligence have to be activated to be of any use. It is hardly necessary to quote the great names we all know so well; we know that Albert Einstein was written off as a poor student at school, we're aware that the Beatles were initially turned down many times and that Howard Schultz of Starbucks was rejected for initial venture capital over 200 times. Perhaps more relevantly, here are just a few examples of 'ordinary' people.

'Ordinary' people change their lives, and massively for the better, too

In these examples, for simplicity and privacy, I have changed names and changed some details. The intent is to show you that real people like you and me can change their lives – if they so wish – dramatically for the better. Here I describe each person's role and the changes that were made using the concepts of the LifeCompass. Of course, I use the term 'ordinary' here in the sense of not being famous. These people are clearly just as important and interesting as the 'brand names'.

Jeremy, technical director

Jeremy was very senior in the organization in which he worked; he had worked his way up from the shop floor and was proud of the position he had achieved with only a minimum of college education. However, he was simply doing too much and consequently was delivering poor-quality thinking, was not seeing his children as often as he wished and was regularly falling ill. His challenge was that he found it very difficult to let go, worrying that if he did so, a younger person might get his job. Eventually, as it became clear that his marriage was breaking down, he decided to get some one-to-one coaching. With that support, he was able to re-invent himself. He used the LifeCompass concept to re-establish the balance between work and the rest of his life. He has successfully rebuilt a strong bond with his children, created clear boundaries between work and everything else in his life and started a workable fitness routine.

Tim, graduate trainee

Though initially aggressive and cynical in the workshop I was running, Tim began to buy into the ideas as they began to reveal a practical solution to some of his problems. After initially focusing on work as something which simply enabled him to clear his debts, he found a genuine motivation for it and decided to set new, higher personal standards for himself. These included giving up smoking and getting his earlier student debts under control. The LifeCompass gave Tim a structure for this process.

Pauline, middle manager

After consistently receiving poor feedback from her teams about what was, in essence, her 'control-freak' style, Pauline used LifeCompass to establish a more credible leadership approach. She had tried many times before, but now realized that she had simply been trying to bolt skills on to the rest of her approach. LifeCompass helped her to take a more fundamental perspective, to forget techniques and instead to live and breathe the concepts. Basically she realized she could only lead others once she could lead herself.

John, middle manager

He'd 'been there, done that': car, house, family, money and love affairs. In his case, LifeCompass led him to the one thing he was lacking – a contribution to something greater than himself. He admitted that this gave him the buzz he was missing. And yet for so long, as a 'committed cynic' (his own words), he had felt that tough guys did not get involved in the caring, sharing side of things.

Janet, mum

For Janet, every stage had been hard. It had been hard giving up her prestigious job in the City to care for her children when she decided that being a mother was more important to her; hard to fund the change in lifestyle; hard dealing with her husband's initial unhappiness at her giving up her job and the consequent drop in household income; hard coping with the view that some sectors of society had of her not working. Understanding the LifeCompass was a revelation.

Juan, technical consultant

Juan had a very poor lifestyle. Although glamorous in one sense – he regularly travelled all over the world – he was also chronically tired, ill and overweight. After some clear thinking on the mind/body compass point, he lost four stones in one year. His health, energy and fun were raised to new levels. His life was fantastic again.

Susan, receptionist

Susan had been a receptionist ever since she left school and had always wanted to be something more. But she wasn't at all sure how. Strategic Edge's Personal Excellence programme was running where she worked but she wasn't allowed to go on it, so she bought a copy of *Being the Best* instead. The LifeCompass showed her that there was no reason why she couldn't step up to a marketing role and also helped her see how to do it. Eighteen months later she became a marketing consultant.

We'll look at more examples in mini case studies as we explore each of the compass points.

Will it work?

Ultimately, change can only happen when an individual decides to take responsibility and make it happen. Please make sure you understand that one point; you must take responsibility for the change you want. However, I've been in the business of teaching and developing people for most of my working life. I've been doing it in a very focused sense for the last fifteen years. And I know these ideas work. How? Well, the LifeCompass has worked for me and for so many delegates that I have taught on so many courses, many of whom have stayed in touch: I regularly receive emails from those who have at last made the changes they wanted to make. I'm delighted to be their catalyst. It will work for you. Take personal responsibility and decide to make it work for you. I believe any blocker you identify – and I don't underestimate the ones you personally may be facing at the moment – can be overcome.

My own story in a nutshell

And in case you think 'hey, that's easy for you to say', to get to the life I wanted I needed to do many things. Firstly I had to make the decision to manage my own destiny. Up until that point it had been tempting to blame circumstances. But, of course, circumstances will never be ideal; it's what you do with circumstances which makes the difference. I also had to recover from a life-threatening, debilitating illness. As well as taking out two months of my life, the side effects remained for years. Then I faced a lack of financial support from the bank in a dire trading climate; I started my business as we went into some of the worst trading times for a service organization. Additionally I needed to manage a considerable personal and financial debt in order to get the business I envisioned off the ground. Finally, I had to deal with the full range of challenges in running a small start-up, from government red tape to employee difficulties. At the same time I continued to give all my love and support to my family who were, after all, one of the reasons I was doing it! I don't mention any of this to impress; I mention it to clarify that while we all have our challenges, we can overcome them.

Personal responsibility

Key to making it work is taking personal responsibility – taking decisions (however small) and consequently actions (however small) that create the changes which you seek. Of course, I'll give you lots of ideas an how to make that process as easy as possible.

Life's a lot easier with a compass

With a geographical compass, there are four essential compass points: north, south, east and west. At a particular location and at a particular time, travelling towards a specific compass point will give specific results. Perhaps, for example, if we travel north we might get to work and if we travel west we might get to a pleasant holiday location. Obviously if we need a holiday then it doesn't matter how fast we travel north; we are not going to get that holiday. And however attractive west might be it would be unusual to want to spend all our time there.

Clearly, choosing the right direction is important, but also getting the right direction at the right time and right pace or balance is vital too. It is exactly the same with our personal development. Direction is key, balance is key. That's what our LifeCompass is for, to support our key life decisions. Decisions such as:

- *Where do I take my career next? And how do I do it?*
- *We've started a family, how can we be excellent parents?*
- *I've got some new exciting work responsibilities. But I've also got a new baby daughter I want to spend time with. How do I do it?*
- *I love being fit. And I love working hard and getting the rewards. What's the 'correct' balance?*
- *I want to take my team forward and I know that that is going to require a lot of time commitment. But I really need to invest in myself otherwise I'm going to*

burn out. Plus I need the executive team to notice me if I am going to get the directorship I want in a couple of years. How do I do it?

- *Where's the fun anymore? I don't just mean going down the pub …*
- *I love the world of business but I feel I am increasingly in conflict with some of the values being expressed by our senior management team.*
- *What's it all about? Whenever I get promotion and my next, bigger car, the buzz goes even more quickly. There must be something more to it that that.*

In LifeCompass, there are six potential areas of focus and attention. These are the compass points. They can be addressed in any order: as they are supportive and synergistic, there is no priority to them. Let's get an overview – simply for convenience let's look at them in this order:

Career

How we earn our money, how we contribute to society, how we fill much of our time, how we grow. How we reveal our creativity and true potential. Quite! Perhaps you had never thought there was so much to simply going to work? Let's give it some attention. Imagine if your career was something about which you were absolutely passionate? Wouldn't that cause a lot of other issues to fall away? Wouldn't many stress-related health issues solve themselves because you would simply feel so much better? And wouldn't a lot of the finance issues resolve themselves because there wouldn't be the same need for so many 'treats'? Wouldn't simply being more fulfilled address the significant issue of happiness? Absolutely – that's what we are going to be working on.

Mind/body

The state of our mind/body determines much of the change we will create in our other compass areas. By definition it is fundamental to all that we do. By 'state' I mean our focus, creativity and energy, because that will determine what results we get. Hasn't it got to be true that if we feel great then we'll be able to make the changes that we want? That's exactly what we are going to address.

Finance

Money. Is this too much of a primary driver? Is it a distraction from some things which are more important? What is true wealth and affluence? Why is it that we often notice that those who suddenly acquire loads of money do not necessarily become happier – sometimes the reverse – and those who are good at making money simply do it as a measure, a yardstick? Wouldn't life be a whole lot easier if you knew exactly what you were chasing and how much you needed? Maybe deciding you don't need so much after all?

Relationships

Are they giving joy or pain? How can you develop them so that they are outstanding? What if your most important relationships were all fantastic?

Fun

What's the point of anything if there's no fun in it? How about if you really got that point and did ensure that you were really having loads of fun? Fun that wasn't based around an over-dependence on alcohol or drugs?

Contribution

How about looking beyond the immediate area? Can you measure the satisfaction you might gain from feeling that you have contributed something useful to society? Do you sometimes feel that you would like to do more and that you could do more, given the opportunity?

Each compass point, each direction is initially apparently independent of the others. Thus we can give considerable focus to career (and perhaps only to one aspect of that career – power) and ignore health. But career and health are, of course, not independent of each other; they are highly interdependent. Who would disagree with the fact that a job very much affects both mood and health? This is the concept of the interdependence of the compass points. Similarly, we might realize after a while that while we have been focusing solely on career, our relationships have suffered, our finances are not as secure as they might be and we have certainly not had fun. This is the concept of the integrity of the compass – not pursuing one direction to the detriment of others. Or we might pursue a life of pure fun to make us happy, ignoring our relationships and physical health and realize that the latter are at least significant contributors to our happiness. This is the concept of the compass pointing in the correct direction. The LifeCompass provides correct direction, integrity and interdependence.

At any time as you develop your LifeCompass you'll be focusing on any one of these directions: career, mind/body, finance, relationships, fun and contribution – maybe unconsciously and maybe inappropriately. Of course, no one direction should exclude the others. In reality we'll be seeing that we actually want balance across all of the compass points. So although we do give attention to each of them (for example, 'what do I actually want out of my career?') we also consider the impact on the other compass points ('... and how might this affect my family?'). In essence the analogy of the compass is to set your direction while considering and giving attention to all the compass points.

Getting the results you want and deserve

As with any area of personal development, there is a lot that we might cover. But I believe, from working with thousands of people of different ages, roles, backgrounds and cultures over the years, that I can guess what you want at this stage. You want to make some changes and you want to do it properly, but you also want some results quickly. So this book is about being 'brilliant at the basics' as far as the LifeCompass is concerned. It's about covering the ideas which will give you rapid, high-pay-off returns and be a basis for further developmental work.

Brilliant at the basics

Now it's time to give some conscious attention to each compass point in order to get the results you want. You'll notice that the structure for each compass point is slightly different: well, each compass point is different. I'll do just as I do in my workshops, I'll ask questions which trigger the necessary thinking with the purpose of gaining clarity and deciding actions which will allow you to fulfil that compass policy. I'll coach you through the process of deciding appropriate actions.

At some stage you may wish to come on one of my workshops (you'll find the details at the end of the book). But, please, at the start simply see the power of attention to these subjects. Giving attention is maybe 70% of the solution. It will help you identify the actions which are necessary to get you to where you want to go.

Chapter 3
Compass Point 1: Career

The first LifeCompass point is career. This comes first only in the sense that it is convenient for us to study it prior to the other compass points; it is a route into the details of the compass. Ultimately we will see that it is no more the 'first' compass point than any of the others. The career compass point is concerned with how we earn money, how we spend much of our time each day, how we get that certain satisfaction that comes from a job well done, a way we contribute to society. It is a fundamental source of our personal development and growth … or perhaps not: sometimes it can feel that our work is the one thing holding us back. If only we could win the lottery then we could do what we truly wanted; then, at last, we would be happy …

Well, maybe it's not quite as straightforward as that. However it is fair to say that one of the most important routes to authenticity and consequent fulfilment is to allow our true creativity to be realized and released. By creativity I don't simply mean painting or writing. It might mean being a customer service wizard or a cool parent or whatever: we are all creators. But many of us are stifled or muffled.

Career is, of course, the one obvious compass point, the one clearly distinct part of our lives: so distinct perhaps that it can begin to dominate to the detriment of other aspects, other compass points. Some people, even though they may only be officially working eight hours each day, are certainly thinking about their work all the time. We need to break that pattern and ultimately recognize that we needn't let career become too dominant in the balance of our compass; we simply want it to take its rightful place.

For now, career is an excellent place to start because of the significant time commitment it requires. We spend a large amount of our day in this area and it doesn't matter whether it's in a corporate role, running a beach bar or parenting, it's still our major time commitment. Interestingly, for many this significant time commitment may then equate to work being the most important aspect. However, that's not necessarily the case, as we shall see. One reason for studying the compass is to bring each aspect of our life into its true perspective, its true importance. Time spent on an activity does not necessarily equate to its importance in the big picture.

Our goal, then, is to achieve clarity in deciding how we really want to spend our time, how we really want to earn our money. But do we actually have any choice over the matter? Surely such discussion is pure luxury and might even raise false hopes?

Yes, we do have choice! No to 'pure luxury'! Yet how can it be so? Work is our fabric; our make-up: our work is us. Thus one very important mindset shift to make is to recognize that we do have a choice: we can decide what career we want. It's important to be careful here; this discussion does not necessarily advocate giving it all up, downshifting and teleworking from the deepest countryside. You may find that, ironically, you are even more unhappy (or, of course, blissfully happy) if you make such a change. But this discussion is about the possibility that the life you wish to lead will, in no small part, be dependent upon the career you undertake. For that reason it is due serious consideration. As you do think seriously about it, you will find that you have more scope than you originally thought. It may not be easy to change, but it's certainly not easy putting up with a poor career for the rest of your life. Many of us drift or are 'diagnosed' into a career. Once we reach a satisfactory level of earnings we then get locked down;

we reach a point of ticking along. There's nothing wrong with that, if we are happy with it. However, do remember it has often been said that the enemy of the excellent is the good; this is particularly true of jobs and careers. If what we are doing is just OK and not too painful, we stick at it. But perhaps what we really want to do is actually accessible, if we simply gave it some attention.

But how on earth do we get clarity on what we really want to do? Try this exercise for size: take a moment to consider where you want your career to be in three years' time and write it down.

Notice the word is 'want'. Don't write down a 'have to' or a 'got to'. Go really blue skies and leave aside the financial aspects (we will, of course, come back to this). Simply consider what you really want to be doing. Don't prejudge at the moment. When I'm running workshops, someone will usually ask 'Nick, do you mean what I genuinely want to be doing? Or what I know I will be doing?' The former! Now if you are happy to go off and consider that question, please do so and return when you are ready. Only read on now if you are stuck. Take as long as you like, even a day or two: it's a big question.

What do you think? Could you go off and tackle it or are you reading ahead because you are just being curious about what comes next? Or did you carry on reading because you wanted more support? If so, you'll be like many of us. It's possible that it is such a long time since you've given such a demanding question thorough consideration that you're a little stunned. That's fine. Help is at hand.

Strategies for help

Here are eight strategies which will help you. One, if not several, will work well with your own style and aspirations. And certainly do try all eight. If you have returned after considering your possibilities and feel you have made some good progress, then scan these strategies and see if they can add any further subtleties to your thinking; my experience when working one-to-one suggests that they probably can.

Here is an overview of the approaches and then we will look at them in more detail. As you consider them, acknowledge the following fundamental working assumptions:

- *We can choose our career; many of us have not yet made that mindset switch or maybe we are now ready for the next choice.*
- *It may not be easy initially, but we are doing it for long-term benefits. Much change is hard initially, but there is also much that we can do to lessen the initial challenge.*
- *The first stage is always to get clarity on what we want. Then we can consider its viability and create a transition plan from what we are currently doing.*

A career is not so much about what we do but about what we are and what we become. Increasingly a career will become something we enjoy so much that we do not resent it: we'll no longer spend much of our time plotting how we can get out of doing it or what we would do if we won the lottery, but simply integrate our work with the rest of our life. Actually, it is our life. Here then are those strategies, those approaches. Initially, I will simply overview them.

Approach 1: Getting clarity by removing distraction

We deliberately remove distracters to deeper thinking which potentially stop us seeing what we really want to do. A simple example of a distracter might be money. Many of us choose our position or job because of the money; clearly understandable but not always wise, certainly not in the long term.

Approach 2: Accessing unconscious thinking

In this approach, we attempt to get at what we are really thinking: those powerful thoughts just below the surface. Our top-level thinking is so often dulled by the conditioning of everyday 'busyness' that it often squashes our real thinking and treats it as being unrealistic. You know how sometimes on holiday you have made breakthroughs in your thinking: well, that's what this approach is about. We often get at what we really think by sneaking up on it.

Approach 3: Sensory-rich visualization

When we can genuinely see, hear, and/or feel what we want, it becomes so much easier to achieve it. This approach is about creating that mental model: about making it so real it is accessible.

Approach 4: Mind Mapping®

Mind Mapping® allows us to combine several of the above approaches and also gives us a visual record of what we have achieved. This is then easily converted into a detailed, action-plan approach. Other benefits include the synergy which is encouraged between left and right brain. We'll be using the mind-mapping approach first described by Tony Buzan and developed by him in many books.

Approach 5: In search of flow

Another approach which combines several of the strategies is searching for flow. A flow state is achieved when we deliver our highest quality work and yet do so effortlessly, without specific focus. Athletes often talk about delivering their best performance when they are 'in the zone'. We too can get into this very specific state, described so well by Mihaly Csikszentimihalyi in his book *Finding Flow: The Psychology of Engagement with Everyday Life*.

Approach 6: Preference guidance

Here we use one of the world's most powerful preference indicators to give us some guidance. By a 'preference' I mean a way of interacting with the world which is specific to us. Even if you are not clear what you do want to do and even if you consider yourself to be early in your career, you have undoubtedly discovered ways in which you definitely prefer to work, perhaps on your own or with large teams. That's probably because when you are working in that particular way you're working with your preference.

Approach 7: Acceptance

This is when we realize that we have the ideal career or position. Yes, it does happen! Maybe you're in it now? Or maybe it really doesn't require much of a tweak to get it right? Perhaps the problem is the way you are being managed, that your commute stresses you out or perhaps, unfortunately, that others are making you feel guilty that it's not appropriate or that you should be doing more. Yet you love it, or could learn to love it, if people would just leave you alone.

Approach 8: Data deprivation

More later, in Strategy 8. But if nothing else works, then this will.

We are now going to look at each of these in more detail. As mentioned earlier, if you have returned from your own thinking you may wish to try these too. They may give you a fresh angle: perhaps reinforce your own thinking or expose a different nuance. To get the full benefit, apply the strategy in full.

Strategy 1: Removing distracters in thinking

Here are some deliberately powerful and provocative challenge points: they are designed to get beyond and around your current thinking, to take you beyond the mindset of your current concerns.

Take each challenge point and write your response. It must be written down and it is important that you write quickly, without judging your response. At this stage don't debate the question; just answer it as best you can. Assume that you do have an answer and that for you it feels an appropriate question (even if it really annoys you!).

Challenge point 1: If you didn't have to work to earn money, how would you spend your time?

Go beyond the initial attractions of the endless holiday. Think deeper. Go on. I know it seems crazy, but just imagine the power of that question. Go beyond the superficial responses of doing nothing. And avoid cynicism; hang onto the possibility that this might indeed be feasible. Go beyond the toys you might buy. What would you love to do? How would you really spend your time? This is a remarkably powerful question, and deliberately so. Obviously its intention is to clarify your thinking and remove all barriers.

But maybe you're reacting cynically and saying it is so unlikely that you simply don't want to think about it. Or maybe you are so stumped by the freedom the question offers you that you don't know what to do or write. Decide to be bold enough to step beyond those feelings. Write and continue to write.

Do have a go. Your compass is important to you. I'll be getting you to work hard on this stuff. Don't stay intellectual, get practical. Write long and hard, now. Keep writing until you are exhausted on the topic. When you pause, write '… and one more thing'. Please start now.

Now try these other challenge points. Take the same approach. Treat them as sensible questions, write and write quickly.

Challenge point 2: How would you love to be remembered by society? What was your contribution? What was your impact on this planet?
Again, write long and hard. How would you love to be remembered? Or maybe you don't want to be remembered, in which case what would you like your impact to have been? Keep writing …

Challenge point 3: Sometimes, just sometimes, I see that my real work is …
Complete this sentence: go on, be honest. Sometimes you get a glimpse: what is it? Even in your faintest dreams. I know it's ridiculous, but write anyway.

Keep your responses, you'll need them later. You may wish to go straight to the action stage that follows all the strategies (p.33) if you are keen to make immediate progress, or you may wish to review some of the other strategies. If you are unsure, choose to review the others and don't be concerned if one or two generate conflicting responses; they'll be resolved later. Here's a tip: do take plenty of breaks between working on these strategies; they are brain stimulating. Take regular sips of water, too. Date, number and keep your pieces of paper, or your jottings on your laptop, in one place.

Strategy 2: Access unconscious thinking

Now if you thought that approach was testing, try this one. Take a fresh pad of paper (A4 size) and a pen or pencil. You can use your computer if you wish, but this is an exercise where pen and paper work particularly well. Once you start writing you must not stop until you reach the bottom of the page. As with all of these strategies, the approach is important and the subtleties are essential for getting the process to work.

Write this sentence and complete it: What I really want to do for my career is …

Then write the sentence again and complete it: What I really want to do for my career is …

Continue to do so down the page. Write quickly, don't stop until you have filled one A4 page. Always write the sentence in full. Don't write ditto marks and don't print out a word-processed template for completion.

Once you have reached the bottom, turn over and write 'My insights are …' followed by the numbers 1 to 20 and write as many insights as come to mind. Try very hard to write something by all the numbers, even if you notice there is some repetition.

Now repeat the exercise! Yes, I am serious. The same starting sentence with a fresh sheet of A4 paper. Keep your hand moving across the page: write quickly. You'll probably find that initially you get a lot of rubbish, repetition, complaining and buts. But then you do get to some valuable stuff.

Hang on to it, and take a break and then move on to another strategy or go straight to Actions, as before, if you so wish. As always, date your work and keep it safely.

Strategy 3: Sensory-rich visualization

In this approach we create a new mental model. We imagine a time, say a year from now, when we are established in our new role. We detail what we are seeing, what we are feeling and what we are hearing. Notice the use of the present tense. What we are seeing, what we are feeling, what we are hearing.

Here's an example. Kathy had a telephone-support role at one of the premium banks. She loved the work but really disliked the environment. Her colleagues were cynical about what needed to be done and tried to get rid of callers as quickly as possible, and her team leader was a bully. But Kathy knew that she was excellent at helping customers. And once engaged with her customer's conversation, however challenging, she loved it. If she could just take that conversation, the interaction part, and drop the rest then her work would be brilliant. Initially she taped her visualization and then transcribed it; this is a neat approach as it allows you to work at the highest speed. Here's what she wrote, as she wrote it, for her sensory-rich visualization:

> *'I see an excellent team around me. I know they are excellent from the big things such as I notice they are keeping up-to-date records but also smaller things such as when someone arrives in the morning they say "hi" to the others around them. I feel a powerful camaraderie in the team but equally no expectation of having to spend social time together. We are talking about our clear goals: I love the fact we have drawings of those goals all around us and we hit them. And when we hit them, we do celebrate with some shouting and jumping around the place. When we don't there's real energy to decide what went wrong and resolve it for the future. I'm on the way to being a team leader; I see senior managers discussing my capabilities and my progress with them and I'm revealing some excellent thinking. I love learning.'*

Now for Tim. Tim loved numbers; he loved making them work, showing how profit was being made or not made, but he was expected to be a team player all the time and he really disliked that bit. Here's his sensory-rich imagery:

> *'I am a consultant. I feel really good about that: I know it's an old-fashioned word, but I feel professional and have absolutely no qualms that I charge high fees for minimum time. I see myself talking to clients and explaining in brilliant terms what needs to be done. I see that I always resolve a client's problems. I*

see myself engaged in short, sharp meetings. I am in high demand, so that I certainly don't need to step lightly when working with the client: I can be direct and ultimately I'm appreciated for that. I love the focus of producing an excellent client report which I know that they appreciate.'

Now let's hear from Karen. Karen is 'high-powered: baccalaureate, Oxford, MBA'. But she hated the corporate life. She knew that plenty of her friends enjoyed it, but for her it was shallow with no spark, soul or passion. How did her visualization go?

'I am a mother and I see myself as a mother. I'm wearing practical and sloppy stuff which allows me to get down on the floor and play games. I love being a mother and in the background I am enjoying researching my second career, although I have no idea what it will be. I enjoy that fact. I am currently working through Julia Cameron's book The Artist's Way: A Course in Rediscovering and Recovering Your Artistic Self *and already am getting some great inspiration not only for me but also for how I can help the children with their own development. I love writing and I love seeing my notebooks filling up. I love the feeling that my children are just growing and developing in such a healthy way.'*

What we really want to do here is get below the organized, conscious, approval-seeking mind and see what the powerful unconscious thinker has to reveal to us. To do that we must write in order to expose our thoughts and, secondly, write in the detail that I call sensory-rich. This enables us to create that new world and begin to really plan. So have a go:

- *Grab an A4 sheet of paper and a pen.*
- *Imagine your 'future state', the place that you want to be.*
- *Write what you are seeing and are hearing and are feeling.*
- *Keep everything in the present tense.*
- *Be wild – that is, uninhibited – in your writing.*
- *Tip: describe what you are seeing, hearing and feeling.*

Strategy 4: Mind Mapping®

A Mind Map® (in this context; there are other uses for a Mind Map®) is an opportunity to access the innermost workings of the mind in a structured manner. Tony Buzan has done a significant amount of work in this area and is certainly an author to pursue for further thinking and resources. For our purposes, you need:

- *45 minutes of time dedicated to this.*
- *A quiet spot.*
- *Some A4 blank paper, which you use in landscape format.*
- *A couple of coloured pens.*

To start Mind Mapping® around your career:

- *Draw a simple picture which represents your career quest in the centre of the paper.*
- *Allow the main ideas which you associate with that to flow: write them on one word per line.*
- *Ensure line length matches word length.*
- *Make the text size diminish towards the edge of the paper.*
- *Important – let your ideas flow: do not plan them logically.*
- *Keep working by moving quickly.*

Work for about 45 minutes then stop and put your map aside.

Figure 3.1 is an example which will help if you need clarification. Please use this only for understanding what a 'real' Mind Map® looks like, not as an example of a perfect one or a correct one.

Take a good break, then come back. You'll probably want to add some ideas and/or lines, or you may want to tear it up or do a redraw. Remember that Mind Maps® are often messy on their first drawing. If you feel like redrawing, go ahead.

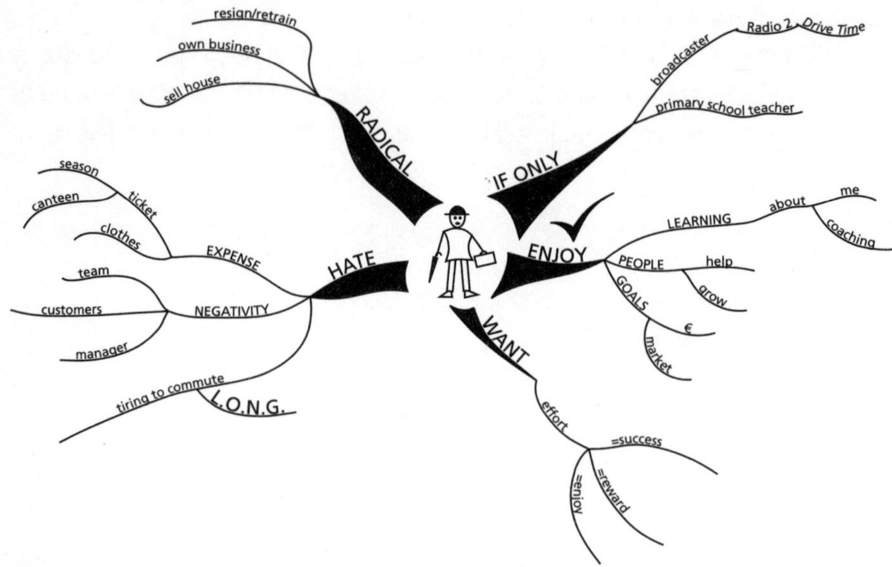

Figure 3.1 The Mind Map®
(Mind Map® is a registered trademark of the Buzan Organisation, used with enthusiastic permission)

Now spend a little time considering it – do any interesting points come out of it? Do you want to reflect on something a little longer? What's the essence of your Mind Map®? Are there any surprises on where the balance of your Mind Map® is? When you do feel that you have the true essence, make that the centre of a new Mind Map®. Then start again.

Strategy 5: In search of flow

In your job, at what points do you get into a frame of mind where you are really enjoying your work? That presentation? Those figures? Dealing with the irate customer? These are points where you are simply not aware of time, where you realize you have done the job brilliantly but you didn't need to refer to any notes. If you basically enjoy your work, this may happen a lot of the time. If you don't, really, then it may happen only occasionally or perhaps when you get a rare chance to cover someone else's job.

What we are searching for here is flow state. Flow state is when you achieve a powerful period of energy and consequent productiveness and enjoyment without apparent effort, without struggle. It's a good indicator of what you might perhaps consider doing full time. Here we go.

When working, which aspects do you really enjoy? But do you really enjoy solving customer problems? Which aspect? The function issue or the people stuff? Do you ever go into a flow state, when mind and body are truly one and you are working very effectively? This might seem a bit esoteric, but when have you been lost in your work? Totally involved and enjoying it? Do you have a hobby that might become a job? Of course, you'll realize that this is one to be careful with – many hobbies do not scale up to a full job.

So think. When do you get lost in your job? What are the fun aspects? When does time flow? When do you feel you have really contributed? At which points do you offer exceptional skill?

Strategy 6: Preference indicator

In this approach, you use a recognized diagnostic indicator which will give you feedback on your behavioural/personality 'preferences': by this I mean your preferred styles of learning, working and relating to people. Knowledge about these can be tremendously helpful in deciding which way to take a career. A few caveats, however:

- *Choose your diagnostic carefully. What is its pedigree? Why should you be confident in the results? If you have any doubt, use the Myers Briggs Type indicator or MBTI (there is more on this later, in Compass Point 4, p.91).*
- *Remember that such information about you is not intended to label you, but to free you.*
- *If you are reading this in the UK, try www.opp.co.uk; otherwise search for recognized MBTI providers in your area.*

Strategy 7: Acceptance

For many people, the career/job/role that they are actually in is not the one which is best for them. It is not the one which gives them passion. But, ironically, some people love their jobs even though few will support them, even though other people feel they should be doing more or something else, saying things like 'you shouldn't have to accept just being an accountant' or 'you'll soon get fed up staying at home with a baby'.

Think a while – is this the career for you? If so, accept it. Do not be influenced by others. One huge benefit of doing these exercises is that it can put in proportion the work you are doing and get you to appreciate it after all, or at least help you make a few tweaks which will ensure that it is more enjoyable.

Strategy 8: Data deprivation

You'll have noticed how all of the above techniques require us to be busy doing something. This last strategy is totally brilliant; we need do nothing... but not a 'lazy' nothing, more an 'active' nothing. It plays to the fact that much of the time we are totally overloaded with data and information; consequently we find it difficult to get out much of our deeper thinking.

So try this: for at least four hours, and the longer the better, deprive yourself of external data. In particular:

- *Get rid of noise: switch off the radio and TV. Get as far away as you can from traffic noise.*
- *Email: leave it for a day.*
- *People: don't set up any meetings.*
- *Reading: ignore the newspapers and your favourite thrillers.*

How can you expect it to go? Initially you will probably be very frustrated. Questions will flood into your mind about just how irritating this is and how much time it is wasting. Go with it, you will eventually begin to notice the powerful benefits. Your own thoughts will begin to surface. Bear in mind that you will probably feel frustrated at first; you may even feel angry. But again, do hang on in there.

Eventually, after a significant period of data deprivation, jot down some thoughts. You will get some fresh thinking.

Whose compass?

In a moment we are going to move into creating actions, but before we do that, perhaps I should anticipate a question which sometimes comes up: 'Do I even need a personal compass?'. Sometimes individuals in my workshops will comment that they don't want to have a plan, never mind a 'whole compass'. Well, ultimately this is your choice. However, do bear in mind that if you are not using your own plan then by default you're using someone else's plan, perhaps that of a teacher or parent or adviser or boss or whoever. Thinking and reflecting and setting your personal compass does not label you. Nor does it limit you. Quite the contrary: it gives you more options. That is the sole reason we're considering it: in order to give you the freedom you seek. Don't dumb down your life.

Actions

Enough of reflection; time for action. And if you have been good enough to resist diving into conclusions and action you have done well. If you have pursued several of the strategies you have done particularly well. Remember that this is not a one-off exercise. Now that you know the approaches and strategies, you can go back to them at any stage. You have not used them up. We'll take each strategy in turn. Here are some specific actions/insights from the eight strategies.

Actions/Insights: Strategy 1 – Removing distracters

So, what did you come up with? Here are some possibilities after your deliberations:

- *Example 1: I'd like to be doing exactly what I'm doing now.*
- *Example 2: I want promotion.*
- *Example 3: I just want to be working somewhere else.*
- *Example 4: I really don't know.*
- *Example 5: I'd love to but I don't think …*

If you've come up with a clear goal, perhaps like one of the first three examples, write down three actions which would take this goal further. Make sure that one goal is to be achieved this calendar month, and two in the next six months, to bring that conclusion to reality. So if, for instance, you wrote down 'to be promoted', what exactly do you need to start doing? For example:

- *'I'll talk to my manager about what exactly I need to do to achieve promotion.' (And note a date by which you will do this!)*
- *'I'm going to book myself on a development programme so that my skills are strengthened.' (Note when!)*
- *'I need to complete these specific goals to this specific level.' (Note when!)*

Work on these actions until you start noticing progress. Remember that in this busy, busy world not everyone will have the time for you that you might like. Some will ignore you, some will be too busy. Be persistent. If someone says no, remember that this simply means no, not now. Be aware of how many people will give you their party line and remember how many of these are Catch 22s: for example, to be a marketer you must have marketing experience; to be a manager you must have management experience. Push around these barriers. Ask for trial runs. Ask for part-time experience. Ask people who are doing what you want to be doing how they got that role. Notice the very important aspect of attitude. Importantly, do not let anyone stop you, do not give up on what you are looking for. If you really want that promotion, then you will get it.

If you don't know (as in Example 4 above), write down how you could begin to find out. For example:

- *'I have loads of friends in other businesses, I could talk to them for ideas.' (Note who and when.)*
- *'I'll read some biographies, such as Anita Roddick's* Business as Unusual.*' (When will you buy it, when will you read it?)*

Support this by the other strategies. Remember that if you have used a process and you didn't get the results that you were looking for on one particular day, it doesn't mean that the process isn't for you or that it isn't working. Leave it and come back to it.

Now, if you don't know, is it that you don't know and don't care? Then OK. But if it is don't know and would like to – and I guess that is the case otherwise you wouldn't be reading this book – then decide to give it some attention. Look for inspiration from friends or career management books or biographies or experimenting in new fields or all of those. And keep working the eight strategies. It is only a matter of time.

If you came up with something like Example 5 – you do know what you'd like to do but you simply feel it wouldn't be possible – go straight to the 'what next?' section, after the actions/insights for Strategy 8. You may find the early part helpful.

And if you haven't yet answered the question or were not honest with yourself, do so now. I agree; it's not that easy. That's why some people never get around to it and then bemoan their apparent lack of success. If you feel really stuck, again go to 'what next?' for some inspiration.

Mini case studies

The thing which stopped Ellen in her tracks was 'Sometimes, just sometimes, I see that my real work is …', because she wrote so easily, and so freely in response, 'to support and help people when they are having difficulties; I get such a buzz from that. It removes me from my own troubles, it makes me feel absolutely worthwhile'. Now, Ellen clearly needs to do more work to get further clarity, but most importantly she has got the initial breakthrough she was looking for.

For Jeremy, it was the amazing, clarifying realization that his work was good, was enjoyable and that there were clearly other areas of the compass he needed to do further work on. When he clearly thought about it, when he put it in context, when he relaxed, when he thought about it, his work was OK.

Actions/Insights: Strategy 2 – Access unconscious thinking

So often we know exactly what to do if only we can get the time to get to the heart of the matter. You'll have discovered this many times for yourself: give yourself a bit of time and space and you 'know' exactly what needs to be done. This process does just that. Once you have written and written, collect your jottings and leave them in a safe place for at least 48 hours. When you return, analyze them carefully: look at what thinking was revealed. Ensure you get right down to the bottom of the page. What were the final comments, how did they compare with the earlier ones? What actions can you take?

Mini case studies

Sue could no longer hide what was there. It just came out, line after line – she wanted a senior job in the consulting firm where she worked. But she knew at the moment, because of her introverted demeanour, she was going to be overlooked again unless she got organized. Her desire was so strong; the worry was how long she had hidden it from herself. She loved this technique: her pencil moved faster and faster as she flew down the page.

Jeremy found this stage confirmed Strategy 1.

Juan found he kept writing that he needed challenge. Clearly he needed to spend more time examining his motivations. Maybe one of the other approaches would help him. This one was frustrating him a bit; there was something there but he didn't seem to be able to get it out.

Actions/Insights: Strategy 3 – Sensory-rich visualization

Take the visualizations, the mental models you have created as far as you can. For instance you have described a world in which you feel you are making a difference. In what way are you making a difference? How, specifically? What are you seeing, what are you hearing, what are you feeling? The more precision you get, the more you develop a particular neural pathway in the brain, the more you get the brain to begin to work out connections and see how this might actually begin to work for it. So, as far as actions go:

- *Stretch the mental model as far as you can.*
- *Consider the mental model which you have described as your end goal. Now work backwards and imagine the steps which are necessary to reach that point.*

You'll remember Kathy, Tim and Karen and their powerful visualizations which we looked at in Strategy 3. Kathy decided to look for a new employer, knowing that when she went for interview she had a very clear picture of what she was looking for. Tim decided to start his own consultancy. His first success was to sell himself back to his old organization so that he had a guarantee of two days' work per week for at least six months. Karen loved her visualization; she knew it was absolutely her. Buoyed up by her feeling of its 'rightness', she bought herself a laptop for her writing.

Actions/Insights: Strategy 4 – Mind Mapping®

Keep the mapping going. Let the ideas flow. Take a few breaks in the process and decide if there is anything which you want to add. Eventually when you feel you have done enough, analyze your Mind Map® line by line and capture thoughts and insights.

Mini case study

Peter's Mind Map® was unexpected. It was meant to be a map of his career, but it became obvious that his family was very prominent and clearly on his mind (it isn't for everyone). After some thought he felt he could combine his expertise and his wish to be nearer his family. He decided to go into more of a consultancy role and get a six-month dedicated contract from his current employer.

Actions/Insights: Strategy 5 – Flow

Experiment if at all possible in your current job/role. Slowly but surely develop more opportunity to do 'in the flow' work. Does it still appeal? Or was it a novelty?

Mini case study

Alberto realized he was a presenter – but even more than that, a performer. He loved being the centre of things, being in front of people. And he had a love of music. He decided to get out of IT and into the event management business.

Actions/Insights: Strategy 6 – Preference indicator

Slowly, surely move towards a job/role which enables you to work to your preferences. Step beyond the confines of your job; begin to design your life so that it supports the style which you seek.

Mini case study

A breakthrough for Lucy was to realize that it was fine to be an introvert. All her life people had labelled her as too introspective, too quiet, even 'not a team player'.

Actions/Insights: Strategy 7 – Acceptance

Have the courage to accept what you enjoy doing – ignore the other stuff which people throw at you.

Mini case study

Before doing anything rash – which he admitted he'd been close to doing on several occasions – Pierre decide to take a long break. He realized that a lot of the problems he was facing were of his own making, and whatever way he looked at it they were going to stay with him unless he sorted them. So that's what he did. And he then discovered he actually enjoyed his current job!

Actions/Insights: Strategy 8 – Data deprivation

Allow yourself to just be without input for a while, without feeling you must read another book on finding the perfect career. Note what happens, what thoughts occur to you.

Mini case study

Tom decided to stop pressurizing himself with having to come up with the perfect career idea. He did decide that he was going to spend some time every week thinking about his career and how it was progressing. At the very least this would help him tremendously with his reflective intelligence but, more than that, perhaps it would give him some inspiration with his career challenge.

What next?

Analyze all of your ramblings from the above exercises. Review them bit by bit, pulling out helpful thoughts and sound bites, and create actions.

You should now begin to feel that you're making progress and that's because you're taking action. Before you go to the next level of detail, consider the following. These are the distillations from my work with thousands of individuals over the years who have been through the process you are going through. Here are the more generic points, not specific to particular strategies.

Decide to give your career serious attention. No one can give it your level of tender loving care. With regular careful attention, slowly but surely your career will be transformed into the one which you are seeking. It may take weeks, months or even years – but it will happen.

Realize that you can do anything you wish. But you can't do everything. Any blocker to the progress you are seeking will be a mental one: develop a possibility mindset. This is not a naively positive one, but one in which you remain resourceful, 'can do' and decide to drop your victim mentality. To take an extreme example: OK, so clearly you didn't want to be made redundant, but given that you are – what can you do?

But surely, you say, I cannot be an astronaut? No, I respond, but do you want to be one? No, comes back the reply – and that's the point. You'll only dream to do what you can do. We're nurturing your nature because somewhere along the line it got squashed. If you have a genuine yearning to do so, then you can be a DJ for example, but you'll need to put some effort in to get there.

Once you are giving your career attention, then decide to step up to the next level and actively manage your career. Very few people do so. Decide to do it as from today. Nobody else will manage your career; not your company, not your career guidance specialist (no, not even them, not to the level you want). It's down to you. And once you do, your career becomes even more exciting and rewarding.

By manage your career I mean:

- *Decide specifically what you want to do with your working hours and continue to do so. Explore questions such as how many hours you want to give to earning money, to your family, to yourself, to others.*
- *Decide not to be held back from anything you want to do. When that sneaky limiting belief appears, put it aside and ask 'What am I serious about here, what am I idly pursuing and what is a great fantasy?'.*
- *Read intensively about your field. Ensure that you keep up to date and that you are seen as a specialist in the area.*
- *Spend time with the experts in your field. Develop your skills so that you are certainly in the top 5%. Why? Well, it's more enjoyable and you will certainly be more employable.*
- *Realize you can get the skills/qualifications you need. Because to get these all you need to do is change your mindset and that is fully under your control. Also realize that, generally, the most desirable quality is always attitude.*
- *Shift from career as something you do to something you are, your passion.*

I mentioned the importance of mindset. Limiting beliefs can stop us from following our career dreams. Many of us have been conditioned to think about 'proper jobs' like the law, teaching, medicine. These are, of course, valid and exciting and, for the right person, satisfying. But what about building boats? Or Ayurvedic medicine? Or running a small café or a bed and breakfast? Apparently, many of us believe 'I couldn't do that'. But if you really want to (and it's not just an idle fantasy) you can. Some people sense an immediate barrier (perhaps to becoming a director) and therefore decide there are things they cannot do: 'Everyone says I need a science A level so …' Or some believe in the 'deferred life plan': work hard, put up with anything because one day … Start to become aware of the limiting beliefs that hold us all back. Yes, of course there are real physical limitations. However, those mental limitations are invariably a lot lower than the physical ones. Let's explore some of those limiting beliefs in more detail.

'I ought to get a "proper" job.' Well, what is meant by the term 'proper'? Do those who make this comment mean that there is a more valid job or a better paying one or one whose name they would recognize, or what? A job is 'proper' when you enjoy it. It allows you to earn the money you need and it fits within society's expectations. When you see this definition you realize that there is a lot more open to you. And how about this term 'ought'? According to who? Your mother? Society? The government? How about you? What do you want?

'Everyone tells me that I will need an MBA.' Well, you know what, get close to the real decision makers. An MBA is essentially about knowledge. What you can bring into play is your attitude. Much of that real knowledge you can learn very very quickly. How about being bold: on your CV put 'virtual MBA' and when asked, be very happy to explain what you mean by that.

'One day it'll be a lot easier.' Why should it? A very important realization is that if you want things to be better, you need to get better. And, anyway, why wait? Start now.

Dharma is a Sanskrit word meaning 'life purpose'. This reminds us that we all have a purpose in this life. Find it and you'll enjoy it and be well paid for it. Let this idea flow – maybe there is something you are really good at, which you totally enjoy and could be well paid for doing. And you're probably en route to it now. But how much closer could you get? Decide to take some time out to explore the earlier questions – 'What do I really enjoy doing?', 'What puts me in a flow state?' and 'Even if I were financially independent, what would I wish to do?'

Decide to be outstanding now. Sometimes people think 'I'll give of my best when I've got my new job/I'm promoted/I'm not so tired'. No, do it now. Make 'outstanding' your new wired-in calibration. But how do you do that? How do you do that when you are having a bad day? When you are not enjoying your work? By looking for the best in the situation. By deciding to get something from it regardless. Then you'll be well-positioned when you do start.

Begin to really enjoy your job. Yes, now. Now is the time to do what is necessary. Once again, wire-in high standards so that they become your norm. They don't require self-discipline because they are routine. Keep this thinking separate from money. We want to make a definitive distinction between work/career and money. Focusing solely on money will possibly send you down the wrong career path. We'll be looking at money later.

No positive change can occur without action. Thoughts, discussion, reading are all great things. However obviously tough it might be, things only happen once we take action.

Time spent does not necessarily equate to importance. Urgent is not the same as investing. You will need to decide to give consideration to your career.

Revise!

Now, revise your earlier actions. Write them down. This compass point has a more involved structure than the others and there is a need to revisit your early actions.

Before moving on take pen to paper or fingers to keyboard and decide what actions you are going to take now: write them down. Distinguish between a decision – like 'I will work on my dharma' – to the action associated with it (for example 'I will read the first chapter of Laurence Boldt's *How to Find the Work You Love*.'). With large decisions/

actions, break them down into smaller components; try as far as possible to break them down into chunks which are both time and mind friendly. Finally, date stamp your action list. Now keep this list clearly visible.

Questions and answers

Is this dangerous stuff – beginning to believe that we can have the life that we want? That we can be a DJ or a doctor or whatever? Surely we aren't all able and how can we all realize our dreams?

Let's take the latter point first. When people state this concern, they are perhaps imagining that everybody will want to realize the same dream, and that is not the case. You may find it very attractive to be running a smallholding in Scotland, but not everybody does. True dreams are very specific. As for ability: to realize a dream we need competence and that extra something. And, as we all know, that extra something is the thing which can make the difference.

What happens if I fail?

You won't fail. You can't fail, because there is no failure: only learning about yourself and how you are progressing. You will simply learn a lot more about realizing the dream you have. What we typically see as failure is merely a setback on the way. We need to look at the bigger perspective and the wider picture. Failure is not giving ourselves the chance to live our dreams.

I feel frustrated with my job but whatever approach I try – and granted yours have been helpful – I just don't seem to be able to get the inspiration I need as to my true 'dharma'.

Recognize that you do have a sense of unease. You know something is up and that you do need to address it. However, given that you are in a state of frustration – and I sense from your question that you have perhaps been in it for sometime because you don't seem to be getting the answer you require – you many need to notice that you have become a little 'dulled'. A useful strategy is to go on a retreat and attempt some serious data deprivation. If you are able to do something dramatic such as complete day, excellent. If not, just take some time out to think about this topic more on your own.

Summary

This is the compass point on which we will all naturally spend most of our time. However, don't accept simply 'surviving' it or 'putting up' with it. Decide to give it clear, focused attention: you will, then, get the changes you want. Begin to think about what you want as your dharma, your life purpose. Remember that books and films and dinner-party conversation are usually about the more dramatic changes people make: 'She gave it all up and now runs a bed and breakfast in Cornwall'; 'They moved and run a small language school north of Malaga'. That doesn't mean your change needs to be that extreme; it may well be a more subtle one. And, of course, you may be in the perfect job/career, but there are other aspects of the compass you need to address. We'll be moving onto those next.

So, summary steps:

- *Step 1: How do you feel about your career now and for the future?*
- *Step 2: If you feel it needs attention, use any of the eight strategies I have detailed.*
- *Step 3: Implement the ideas which were highlighted by your work on the exercises.*
- *Step 4: Use the bonus section coming up to help with key issue questions such as how you make the transition from where you are now to where you want to be.*

You now have a set of actions. Start work on these. Re-read this section. Pursue the further reading at the end of this compass point. Expand your capability via the bonuses.

Bonus section

Bonus 1

'So, I know what I want to do. And I'm as confident as I think I can be that it will be a successful move. But I do have responsibilities, I do have money issues. How can I (a) be confident that it will work, and (b) make the transition if I am going out on my own?'

Let's take each point in turn. Firstly, one of the greatest points anyone can realize when beginning to manage their own life is that there are no guarantees, there are no ways to absolute security. Funnily enough, even if you have a lot of money, you can still lack security; you may well worry about the money and what will happen if you lose it and how you can invest it in the best way. Realize that no one can guarantee that it can work. Ultimately, having weighed up all the points in favour and against the plan, follow your intuition. That might seem a shocking, irrational thing to say. Well, think back over your life to date. You know how well intuition has worked for you so far. Follow it again here once you have done all your background work. Do remember, on the pro side of your decision is the invaluable feeling of 'following your bliss', of doing what you feel is important to you.

Secondly, here are six things that you might do to manage the transition:

- *Accept a degree of uncertainty and instability.*
- *Get very clear on what you want to do.*
- *Create a simple project plan, a week-by-week plan of what you will do to achieve your goal.*
- *Get your finances in order before you start and keep them in order as you continue. Get your cost base down and do everything you can to get your revenue up.*
- *Ensure you read and understand the basic sales and marketing processes.*
- *In particular understand that it is important to break the connection between time and money. Change it to value and money.*

Bonus 2

'It strikes me that my CV is going to be central to getting the position I want: what makes a great CV?'

Here are three suggestions. Update your CV once a month, even if you have absolutely no intention of leaving your current position. Every month, take a look at it and edit it. Add new experience. Why? It keeps you focused and if you do ever need to use it, it's ready to go. Then get proactive about your career hunt, whether it is inside or outside your current organization (see Bonus 3). Finally ensure your CV is clear, presentable, has no mistakes and is free of ambiguities.

Bonus 3

One way to get the job/career you seek is to hunt for it. A second is to create it.

Firstly, let's look at the proactive career hunt. The tremendous advantage of this is that your CV does not arrive with 200 others. But it must be genuinely focused to the specific organization, to the role you are seeking, otherwise it is only a mailshot. Be courteous. How to do it?

- *Define the job you seek.*
- *Identify the organizations for whom you would like to work.*
- *Identify the names of those who are the decision makers (this is increasingly difficult via reception, but try corporate websites or ring internal departments and ask them).*
- *Networking. Ask every one of your contacts. Be clear to specify what level of confidentiality you seek about the discussion.*
- *Selling yourself: consider yourself as a brand and product. What is special about you? What can you offer?*
- *Argue financially: what return on investment will the company get in return for taking you on? How quickly could you be up and running?*

Bonus 4

We all want security in times of change. But there is no such thing as absolute security – none at all. Many think it will be money, but in fact once you have money you just worry about looking after it. Here is the key: true security is in you – that you are using your talent, you are using it well and consequently you are being well paid for it. Here are the three keys to inner security:

- *Whatever happens you are doing your best.*
- *You are discovering more and more about yourself.*
- *Things will get better: they always do in the long term.*

Bonus 5

'Dharma. I love this concept. It finally encapsulates something which has been "itching" away for ages. But how on earth do I get a handle on it? How on earth do I start working seriously in this area?'

Simply accept it. Accept that dharma, life purpose, is a possibility. We might also define it as that unique 'nurture your nature mix' which is perfect for you.

Reading

Remember, it can take time for clarity to come in these areas. An excellent way of gaining extra clarity is via reading and listening to people speak on these topics. For further reading and inspiration on this topic, try these:

Anything by Joseph Campbell. Joseph Campbell has done some of the most significant work in this area. There are many books and audio recordings attached to his name. Read and listen to him for further ideas.

Laurence Boldt wrote an excellent book called *How to Find the Work You Love*. I know from my workshops that many people have found this to be very influential in their thinking.

Richard Bolles wrote the classic on career management: *What Color is Your Parachute?* Always get the latest edition; it is published each year around November.

My first book, *Being the Best: The A to Z of Personal Success.* This details success in 26 manageable steps. And also by me *JfDI: Just Do It* is great for turning ideas into action.

Many of Tony Buzan's books are useful for more work on Mind Mapping®. Try *The Mind Map® Book*, published by BBC Publications, for example. (The Mind Map® was developed by Tony Buzan and is a concept supplied by Buzan Centres Ltd, 54 Parkstone Road, Poole, Dorset, BH15 2PG – www.buzancentres.com.)

'Follow your bliss.'
Joseph Campell

Chapter 4

Compass Point 2: Mind/Body

Write, in capitals, beside or even better *on* the mirror above the basin you use for your morning wash: THIS MIND/BODY IS ALL I'VE GOT!

This compass point, mind/body, reminds us to give attention to our mind and body and realize they are firstly, and in every sense, fundamental to everything we wish to achieve. How can we achieve anything without energy? Or without an inclination to act? Or without an ability to think clearly and to have the focus and concentration which is necessary to doing a job well and living a life fully? How can we be happy without authenticity? Secondly, it enables us to realize that mind and body are much more strongly interrelated than any of us might initially imagine; even the most sceptical have undoubtedly noticed how often people seem to be more vulnerable to illness when they're feeling low. And surely the power of passion hasn't escaped us? This is most commonly associated with love and romance, of course, but what would happen if we did more things more often with passion? How would it feel? How effective we could be!

If the term 'mind/body/spirit' seems more appropriate to you, then that is fine. It is beyond the scope of this work to look at what many might consider the most fundamental level of this compass point: the spiritual one. All that needs to be said is that none of this is in conflict with the nurturing of the soul or spirit, however we might wish to do that. For those of you who are interested in this area, see the brief discussion towards the end of this compass point, just after the questions and answers section.

Of course, you might have a job and a family and a car, maybe some money in the bank, but it is all dependent upon the state of your mind/body. When you are in 'great state' – when you wake in the morning, saying 'Yes! Another great day', when life's little challenges remain little challenges – you know you can do anything. But when you are in a poor state: well, you will probably know from past experience that nothing great is likely to happen as you attempt to survive the day. Great state is:

- *Excellent focus: the ability to give clear and direct attention to what is important, when it is important, whether that be your son and his desire for some help with his toys or your boss and repositioning her demands for a strategic report.*
- *Excellent energy: the strength and stamina to deliver, to pull through, to ensure everything happens consistently and on time. This is the ability to do what is necessary, even when you don't necessarily feel like doing it.*
- *Excellent inclination to act: this is a fundamental characteristic of those who are able to achieve the success they crave, an ability to lower the resistance to change, an ability to drive down the change threshold. It's also the ability to recondition and request new muscle memory and develop new burnt-in synaptic pathways.*
- *Light-heartedness: an ability to put things in proportion, to realize that in comparison with some of the bigger priorities certain things are not such an issue after all.*
- *Excellent creativity: an ability to look at problems in a new way, to work at things differently using different skills.*
- *Abundance thinking: this is an ability to look at a situation and see what potential it might hold and what good might come out of it for yourself and others.*

So, honestly, are you doing enough to look after your mind/body? Let's do a quick diagnostic: no 'ifs' or 'buts', just honest answers to how you are doing …

- *Are you exercising it so that heart and lungs and muscles are in fantastic condition? And, consequently, so that you have the strength and stamina you need?*
- *Are you fuelling it well, giving it a clean energy source that ensures you feel great all day, every day without recourse to overdosing on confectionary or coffee or cola drinks?*
- *Are you perhaps teaching it a language to stretch its neural network and developing new memory skills, or Mind Mapping® to open up new parts of the mind?*
- *Are you giving it good quality rest, sleep and fresh air so that it will be creative and energetic?*
- *Have you clicked to mind and body being one and realized the enormity of that? Do you understand that how we treat our body will have a significant impact on our mental well-being? Equally, of course, our mental well-being is bound to affect our physical well-being.*
- *Are you able to look back and compare how your mind/body was five years ago and be pleased with development in this area? Are you able to project forward five years and see the changes you will continue to make and how you can be stronger, fitter and more agile?*
- *Or are you a couch potato? A flight of steps leaves you dizzy. Your mind is cynical and closed. Curiosity is something which killed the cat; it's certainly not for you …*

MEDS

If you are committed to caring for and developing your mind/body, both for their own sake and also for the impact they have on the other compass points, you should consider

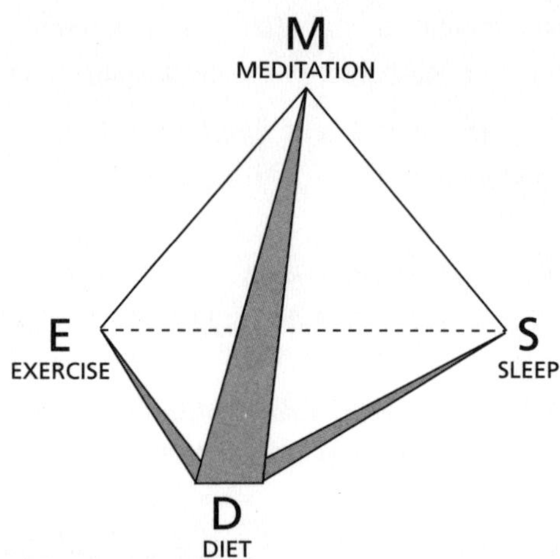

Figure 4.1 MEDS pyramid

your 'MEDS'. MEDS is a holistic and synergistic strategy and the four components are meditation, exercise, diet and sleep. If we show them as four points on a pyramid we can see how they contribute balance and support to each other (see Fig. 4.1).

All four elements are vital: hard cardiovascular activity may well create fitness, for example, but not necessarily balance and certainly not necessarily wellness: note the number of top athletes who have immense health problems later on, or maybe the health food fanatics who cut out many items from their diet and only succeed in being weak and not seeming to enjoy life. A reason that many do not make the progress that they would like on their health and fitness is often because they go overboard on one particular aspect. MEDS is a balanced strategy on all fronts. By tackling all four simultaneously, it becomes a lot easier to achieve our overall goal, which is wellness. I define wellness as an optimal state of physical and mental well-being; we feel good, we feel authentic. Let's take each element in turn.

M – Meditation

Were you a little anxious when you saw this one? Perhaps it conjured up images of incense, robes and chanting? Maybe you leapt immediately to thoughts of what your colleagues might think of your new-found practice? Although meditation is fundamental to many cultures, it is still seen as new to many in the west and, as with so many areas, it has been open to misunderstanding. Our interest here in meditation is purely as a practical fast-track route to great state. Stay open-minded and I am confident that you will add meditation to your personal portfolio of 'unmissable' daily practices. It is not enough on its own, but it is certainly a key component. For many, the day-to-day rush and pressure of everyday life has become close to intolerable; meditation gives a very different alternative to that.

The essence of the concept

Allow yourself to take some time out each day to stop the internal noise, to recharge. This time out might be as simple as taking a walk. As you walk, allow yourself to slow down and reconnect with what is important in your life. Put aside all those concerns that you have for the moment and just decide to 'be', to allow yourself to relax and enjoy yourself. Perhaps learn a formal meditation. For many people, a more formal meditation method is one of the big breakthroughs in their lives, a point at which they finally learn how to build stillness and reflection into their frantic days. For some it happens immediately, for others it takes a little longer. In a moment I'll show you how to do a simple daily breathing meditation, but first do remember that there is nothing overly odd and certainly nothing weird about this practice. The meditative process attracts us because all the evidence shows that in it we are entering a different state – a state which encourages the release of stress and one which can have an impact on factors such as our heart rate. Meditative states are often reached accidentally; watching a beautiful sunset, for example. Doing a breathing meditation allows them to be reached in a more selective way.

In practice

Try and do one for ten minutes each morning and each evening every day. The morning meditation complements your sleep and sets you up for the rest of the day. The evening one ensures that you have a revitalized evening and sleep well. Try and meditate every day at least once. It is a proactive mechanism, a bit like brushing your teeth.

- *To actually meditate, sit quietly in a comfortable, upright chair. Choose a location which will be quiet and undisturbed, but don't try and find somewhere which is absolutely silent; you probably won't, unless you go to a cave in the Himalayas and that's a whole other story! Focus on your breathing and allow your mind to get a little quieter and allow your body to relax. Thoughts will come to mind but return your awareness to your breathing. Don't try 'not' to have thoughts; simply be aware of your breathing (see below).*
- *By focusing on your breathing I certainly don't mean forcing it to take on a particular speed or style: don't try and change the speed or to count the breaths, simply be aware of the in breath and the out breath, and so on. And if you notice a thought or a noise distracts you, return to the flow.*
- *Some meditations will be very relaxing, some very turbulent. It is often the latter which are the most helpful. Try not to judge the experiences you have during meditation, just accept that they are what your mind and body need at that moment.*
- *One more time: don't try and 'not have thoughts'. You will have thoughts, don't fight them. Instead focus on your breathing.*
- *Above all don't worry about what happens during your meditation – it's what happens outside it which is most important. As you meditate on a regular basis you will notice significant change.*
- *Once you can, extend your meditation time from 10 to 15 to 20 minutes a session.*

Some people often feel huge irritation with their meditations. 'Why don't I feel good?' they ask; they'll insist that 'nothing is happening' or will say 'this is stressing me out even more'. That's OK; such feelings are likely to be the release of stress. Sometimes you may find that you are simply falling asleep, in which case sleep is probably what your body craves most. As you continue your meditations they will certainly become more straightforward, generally enjoyable and will undoubtedly be having a cumulative effect on creating a great state.

Mini case study

Sue was a control freak: her description. She always had been; her mother told stories of how as a child she'd been organized about her dolls and clothes to the point of getting very upset if things were out of order. At work this caused her a lot of distress and was increasingly doing so. It was not only her personal inability to let go of stuff and switch off, but also the feedback she got from her own team. Learning meditation was a challenge for her; she wanted to know all the whys and hows of it. Eventually she got the message and realized it was actually quite good for her simply to accept something and not over-analyze it for once – and to realize that despite not necessarily understanding what was happening, it did work. She learnt meditation successfully. She learnt to relax, became more effective at work and restored balance to her personal life. She has increased this way of thinking into her life and has also taken up yoga to complement her meditation. In addition, she decided to take a walk every lunchtime, rain or shine.

E – Exercise

Yes, yes, you know. You've heard it so many times you are sick of it. You know you should be exercising seriously at least three times a week. But, as you consider your body – perhaps a little overweight, perhaps requiring more toning, perhaps looking unwell – you think that it is just an impossibility to get that time in at the gym.

Well, let's get back to the fundamentals. We are not necessarily talking here about going to the gym. This is about exercise: the two need not be linked at all, however ridiculous that might seem. It is probable that the gym is suitable and enjoyable for only a small percentage of the population. We are here concerned with firstly the wellness and secondly the inclination to act that comes through exercise.

In essence

Our body is meant to be used. In fact, it is a real case of 'use it or lose it'. Develop a 'cardiovascular/use my body' mindset. Be aware that society will be against you. Although at one level we are encouraged to take exercise through government policy and colour supplement articles, at another level society very much dissuades us from doing this and makes it difficult. Society encourages you not to use your body. Many factors are subtle and hidden, like not walking to the post but clicking your mouse to send email instead. More are obvious, like the increasing use of lifts and escalators rather than stairs, even for just one floor.

In practice

Take cardiovascular exercise each day. Walk whenever and wherever you can. Take the stairs; notice how society encourages us not to walk. Don't panic and feel that you must use the gym. If you like using the gym then you are probably pretty fit anyway. But if you don't, then think in a Pareto, 80/20 way: for example, 'What 20% of activity will give me 80% of the benefit?'. In addition:

- *Always take the stairs.*
- *Walk further, when safe and sensible; leave your car a little further from your destination and stride out. Get out one tube station earlier. Walk a little further before catching the train.*
- *Practise 'standing', that is don't sit and slump all of the time. Practice standing and as you do, think about your posture.*
- *Set yourself specific but achievable goals, such as 'I will walk briskly at lunchtime*

for 25 minutes whatever the weather'.

- *Once you start noticing energy and stamina kicking in again, think about adding to your cardiovascular repertoire: swimming and cycling are excellent.*
- *Above all, develop a cardiovascular mindset. Think, live and breathe: move!*

Don't accept any excuses. Wherever you are – at home, away in a hotel, in your office – cardiovascular exercise can be taken.

Once your fitness develops, then consider doing simple resistance work. Such work, of course, ensures that our muscles are toned and that we feel great. This is a good reason for getting a couple of free weights, such as dumb-bells, or perhaps a 'stretch-band'. Either way they will ensure that you feel good about yourself and that you have strength to act. Exercise is the factor which we know can cause an inclination to act and it comes very quickly; simply start work and the results come through.

Mini case study

Jon was only 27, but he was seriously unfit. His last significant cardiovascular activity had probably been when he was 14 at school, the last year he had been forced to do sport. But now, still a young man, he'd had a shock. At his company they'd had a charity knockabout five-a-side football competition, and it had nearly killed him. His legs ached but more worryingly he had simply not been able to get his breath. He decided things simply had to change. He started with using every set of stairs at work and when he was away staying in hotels. This was hard the first few weeks but it rapidly became easier and actually enjoyable. A few months later he now swims every other morning, always takes the stairs and walks as far as he can. He feels good and looks so much better.

D – Diet

Much of the challenge with this element of the MEDS pyramid is overcoming mixed messages from so many sources on 'what is good for us' and also on how we should look.

In essence

Diet: not as in going on one, but as in thinking carefully about what we are eating. None of us would put a mixture of diesel, unleaded petrol and sand into a car; it would be crazy. After all we all know specifically what fuel the car needs and what ensures maximum performance, so why break the rules? Yet we often treat our own bodies in an even more bizarre way. A sensible fuel for the body includes complex carbohydrates, fruit and vegetables but minimizes reliance on simple sugars, excess tea or coffee. This is a particularly tricky area, as at any one time there are usually a few new diets being touted about. When evaluating a diet remember, firstly, that any diet will sound initially attractive as it will be different to the one which you are currently on and, secondly, that most diets will get results in the short term; you are looking for something that will work for you in the long term.

In practice

There are, of course, so many different recommendations and there are different body types. However, most would agree with the following:

- *Always involve your doctor in your plans to improve your health.*
- *Keep it simple: complicated rituals are hard with a busy lifestyle.*
- *Keep it enjoyable: food must always be enjoyable.*
- *Balance is critical: more harm than good can be done by going overboard on one particular idea.*
- *Learn to listen to your body: get in tune with what makes it feel good, but do be prepared for slight reactions when you improve your diet.*
- *Integrate this with the other elements. A great diet will not be sufficient on its own; it must be supported by the rest of the MEDS approach.*
- *Follow this simple checklist. Few would argue with these on the positive list:*
  - *Oxygen: the brain is just 2% of the body's overall mass and yet requires 20% of the body's oxygen. Take regular oxygen breaks including a walk around the block and/or simply stretching. Make sure you have a one-minute oxygen break every 45 minutes and a proper 45-minute break at lunchtime.*

- *Water: as we dehydrate fatigue kicks in. Drinking a couple of litres a day is fine for most people. Just sip it during the day; when you feel like a drink, encourage yourself to drink a beaker of water first.*
- *Fruit: this has disappeared from many people's diets, yet it is an essential part of our nutritional spectrum.*
- *Vegetables: the same is true of vegetables; an essential source of vitamins and minerals.*
- *Complex carbohydrates: an excellent source of fuel, long term and satisfying.*

- *Note these on the negative list:*
  - *Sugar: is only a quick-fix energy source, it has no food value and is addictive. It plays far too great a part in many people's diets.*
  - *Caffeine: drink coffee and tea with care. Avoid becoming dependent upon caffeine for 'peak state'.*
  - *Junk food. What is junk food? Anything which is highly processed, anything where you read the label but are still unsure of what is in it. Food you crave but often feel 'down' after eating or until you get your next fix. The good news is that the supermarkets are keen for us to have good quality food, so it is becoming more widely available.*
- *And try this concept to pull your overall strategy together: the calorie triangle. Attempt as far as possible to have your main calorie intake early or earlier in the day than you do at present.*

Mini case study

Tony's biggest challenge was that he felt he genuinely didn't have time to cook fresh food and that was why he depended on a diet of processed meals. After learning more about foods and their impact on his state he made a decision to learn more about cooking; he felt that if he did that not only would he get the benefit of better food, but it would also be great for his mental dexterity. Buying a copy of Nigel Slater's *Real Fast Food* did the trick. He now has a lot more energy, never knowingly eats processed food and loves cooking for himself and others.

S – Sleep

In all my work with a huge variety of different people, of differing backgrounds and ages, this is the one component of MEDS where I find there is most ignorance. Let's be clear: you need your sleep; it is not optional, it is not something you can ditch. And you need sleep of the right quality. Sleep is definitely quantity times quality.

In essence

The first thing to be reminded of here is the powerful social conditioning many of us may have experienced in this area and that is that 'real leaders simply do not need much sleep'. Before we know where we are stories are being repeated about Winston Churchill, Margaret Thatcher and others. The association between great leaders and needing little sleep is not something which should drive our own behaviour. Firstly, much of it is a myth: they were getting their afternoon naps! Secondly, most of us by definition are not on the extremes of the bell curve so we are unlikely to have the extreme genetic ability to do this with which some have perhaps been endowed. Sleep debt occurs when we don't get the sleep which we need. Clearly, when we are suffering from sleep debt we are not going to be able to function at maximum effectiveness or maximum enjoyment. We are certainly not tempted to work on our compass points. Remember: for change, we need space and energy. All aspects of MEDS are clearly critical to the latter.

In practice

What can you do to reduce your sleep debt? Well, it's not necessarily easy and that's why many people don't do it. The key is to start the process and slowly but surely incorporate these ideas into your daily routine:

- *Always wind down several hours before going to sleep. Ensure you have a proper evening. Avoid late-night email.*
- *Avoid stimulants before going to bed, for example caffeine or alcohol. They disrupt sleep patterns.*
- *Keep the bedroom as a place of rest, sleep and love. Avoid turning it into a spare*

room, tip and/or study. Don't sit in bed doing email on your laptop!

- *Try to go to sleep at around the same time each night. Try and wake up around the same time each morning.*
- *Try to wake without an alarm. Set the alarm for ten minutes later as a back-up, but adjust your sleep until you are awaking naturally.*
- *Aim to have around eight hours a night; use that as your benchmark. As you build up your meditation you will find that you need a little less sleep, and certainly your sleep should be of a better quality.*

Mini case study

Pierre was the original action hero and certainly one element of that was (in his view) not wasting time on sleep. Two alarm clocks did the trick followed by a shower and plenty of coffee. The only difficulty was that he was aware that he felt very tired as soon as he stopped. Jet lag hit him very hard and the gym was a particular strain. Coming on a Personal Excellence workshop and learning about the importance of sleep was an incredible revelation for him: he started clearing his sleep debt. He also started feeling great immediately!

Actions

Write down five things that you can do to improve. Not just your mind, not just your body. Here are some examples to act as an inspiration: nothing complex – simply achievable.

1. Walk every day, in particular take the stairs at every opportunity.
2. Eat fruit and vegetables every day, every lunch and/or supper.
3. Drink more water.
4. Learn a language; take a Pareto approach. What about 100 useful words of Italian?
5. Do a crossword.
6. Deliberately read outside your mainstream area. Read about past British Prime

Ministers. Read about the science of tackling AIDS.

7 Use a stretch-band every day to build muscle.

8 Deliberately work hard to understand (not necessarily agree with) someone else's strong viewpoint.

9 Take time out in nature.

10 Take a different route to or from work.

11 Read some poetry: anything from Spike Milligan to Shelley.

12 Learn t'ai chi.

13 Learn to meditate.

14 Learn chess and/or the Chinese game of go.

15 Subscribe to *National Geographic* or *New Scientist* magazine.

16 Learn some Spanish cookery.

17 Take up watercolours.

18 Join the National Trust and visit the places it owns in your area.

19 Learn the Greek and Russian alphabets.

20 Write a mini-book on a favourite topic; it doesn't have to be published.

21 Start swimming again.

22 Don't watch any television for two weeks and, at the same time, don't drink any alcohol!

23 Cancel the newspapers.

24 Read to the children, even if they are teenagers.

25 Read a memory book and learn how to memorize a randomly shuffled pack of cards.

26 Choose a surname. Look it up on Amazon. Read one of their books.

27 During the day make three donations to charities.

28 Book an hour with a personal trainer. Tell them what you want out of a six-month programme.

29 Make contact with an old friend.

30 Write a gag.

31 Accept that lists don't have to end with even numbers!

Insights

Firstly, recognize the mind/body connection. Realize that your mind and your body are intimately linked. What we do to one clearly affects the other. Register that our bodies give us feedback; a headache is not a failing of the mind/body system, it's simply a message that says something like rest, look after yourself, slow down and take a break. Understand that as we strengthen our minds, we strengthen our bodies and vice versa, and as we strengthen our bodies, so we strengthen our minds.

Although we started with career (Compass Point 1) as it seemed a natural place to begin, in fact mind/body is perhaps the base compass point. Without a sound mind/body, how does anything else work? As with all of the compass points, there is so much we might do, but once again simply decide to be brilliant at the basics.

Now, decide *your* actions.

Questions and answers

What about nature/nurture? Are some of us simply genetically limited to what we can do?

The nature/nurture debate has been a long one. This is about whether we are predetermined or whether we have the ability to choose who we are. The percentage degree of influence on either side has oscillated over the years. In history, for example, the Victorians certainly considered people to be 'blank slates' onto which specific behaviours could be written. Most recently, with our significant breakthrough in the understanding we have about the influence of genes, more credence has been given to those who believe in the heavy influence of heredity. We are significantly genetically determined. However, there is still plenty of room for us to choose who we are and what we do. Choice is the issue.

What about different body types? Surely some people are naturally more skinny and some are heavier? And weight distribution can shift significantly at different times of our lives. Can we all really get fit?

Certainly. It's clear when we look around that different body types do occur. These body types have different weight distributions. For a fascinating study of this look at *Perfect Health* by Deepak Chopra. This information will help you go beyond simple ideas like one body type being heavier than another and realize that it has more to do with physiology. Thus some people are much more sensitive to coffee than others, for instance. It is also true that as we get older our body begins to layer mass around our body in different ways, a good reason for starting early with good practices. However, whatever your body type, you can ensure that it is fit, that it is well. But – absolutely – don't make yourself miserable by trying to achieve a body shape which is genetically impossible for you.

With exercise – will I ever enjoy it? Will it always be a duty?

Let's put it another way; if you are not enjoying it, then it is not sustainable. Choose a form of exercise which you do enjoy. Snowboarding is fine for some, not for others. Gentle but long walks through woodlands, while life-enhancing for some, would drive others spare.

How do I know when I am well?

Of course your GP can carry out all the necessary medical tests, blood pressure, etc. But here are some simple ones:

- *Stop and ask yourself how you really feel.*
- *How easy do you find it to wake up in the morning?*
- *Look at your eyes and tongue: do your eyes look sparkling, is your tongue clean and pink, are your eyes dull and red?*
- *Cravings: notice when you can't start the day without a coffee, when you simply must have a bar of chocolate. Such food cravings are often a sign of imbalance.*

Can I become brilliant/a genius?
I am convinced that we all have our own level of genius: true genius might be defined as fully releasing our nature through nurture, given that we each have a unique genetic gift to offer.

As I get older I seem to be forgetting things.
There are two factors here: one is simply that because there appears to be a general belief that we get more forgetful as we get older then we notice the things that will reinforce that belief. The other is recognizing that we must use our memory. Much of technology has made it unnecessary for us to remember things in the way that we once had to, but use your memory instead.

Mind/body/spirit

Some of you may find it more appropriate that I should expand the term mind/body to mind/body/spirit. You may perhaps feel that I don't seem to have got to the heart of true mind–body connecting and true wellness. For those among you, let's just spend a brief moment on that now.

So what do I mean by spirit? In this book, in this context, I am talking about a higher concept which appears to exist for many people. When it is accessed, we notice how much more healthy we feel, what happens to our level of 'luck', the ability of coincidences to work for us and so on. This does not negate or contradict anything which I have talked about so far. And, most importantly, this need not be seen as an 'advanced' topic, only for some people.

Bonus section

Bonus 1: Getting it to happen with Pareto

Of all the compass points, the need for change with the mind/body compass point is so apparent, and yet so tough and elusive. Why? Change so difficult – on any compass point – because we often have to undo years of mental conditioning. Physical change is especially difficult because we are working on conditioned muscles, not just a conditioned neurology. That gives us twice the stretch, twice the workout.

What can we do to overcome this? We can get help from Pareto. Pareto's Law is the 80/20 rule and it is a brilliant way of getting change to happen. This rule reminds us that change is not directly proportional to the effort put in. Thus to start getting healthy you don't need to eat a totally macrobiotic diet, simply drinking more water and eating more fruit would get you started and give significant payback. And that is the point: 20% of effort gives you 80% of return. With mind/body, just use MEDS. Here we don't try and become super-fit or go on a slightly weird diet, we simply work on a single element of the four. Let's see how you might do that with each:

- *Meditation: do ten minutes every morning, ten minutes every evening, every day. Anybody and everybody can find ten minutes.*
- *Exercise: develop a cardiovascular mindset; in other words, look for opportunities to do cardiovascular exercise. In particular take every set of stairs and walk everywhere you can.*
- *Diet: start thinking about your diet and (1) only eat what you have consciously chosen and (2) when you eat it, consciously eat it.*
- *Sleep. Get enough sleep, so that you wake naturally: start by going to bed just half an hour earlier each night.*

Bonus 2: Real food, great taste, really quick

Doesn't great food take a lot of cooking, need a store cupboard, lots of utensils, a commitment to cooking, etc? The simple answer is no. It requires a decision to do it. Get your basic cooking utensils:

- *Something that allows you to grill as an alternative to frying.*
- *A vegetable steamer and a pan.*
- *A couple of sharp knives.*

Get set up:

- *Clear the clutter.*
- *Get a couple of chopping boards, one for vegetables, one for fish and meat.*
- *Get salt and pepper grinders.*
- *Order boring or heavy regular stuff (for example, cereals or bags of rice) on the internet; get it delivered.*

Keep it simple. Make:

- *Grills with vegetables.*
- *Home made soup.*
- *Pasta.*

Finally, read great cookery books, especially those by Nigel Slater.

Bonus 3: MEDS on the road

OK, you say, so how do I do MEDS in a hotel?

- *M is easy. When you get in your room, drop everything on the floor, loosen your clothes if you're still in smart business gear, and do your 10-minute meditation. Immediately.*
- *E: now you'll be feeling a little more mellow. Put away your bags and get changed. Either go for a brisk walk of 20 minutes or a swim or a workout. You choose, but do it.*
- *T. T? Where did that come from? Telephone! Phone home and tell them you love them.*
- *P. P? What's that? Preparation. Any preparation needed for tomorrow? Do 30 minutes, maximum. Now start to wind down.*
- *D: look at the menu in your room and ask (bully if necessary) for simple grilled food. Resist beer and wine. Or walk to somewhere local, or go to the local food hall.*

- *S: wind down for at least two hours; start travelling with good books to read.*

Summary

Mind/body is one of the compass points for two reasons. Of course it deserves its place in its own right: our mind and body need to be consciously cared for. The second reason is that without a 'well' mind and body we have little real inclination to action. As I said, mind/body is perhaps the base compass point. When our minds and bodies are in great state we will begin to achieve everything we wish. When they are not, we are going to have challenges.

Our career compass point is where we do our most fundamental work to set our direction. Mind/body is where we invest to support those changes. Decide now to shift your perspective to mind/body.

Reading

Deepak Chopra: *Perfect Health*, Bantam, 2001.

Martin Seligman: *Authentic Happiness*, Nicholas Brealey, 2003.

Chapter 5
Compass Point 3: Finance

Career is the initial compass point: naturally so. The mind/body compass point ensures it happens: easily, with joy or not. So, where does the finance compass point fit in? As with all of the compass points, at several levels. Our immediate focus will be to ensure that our personal finance, specifically money, does not become a distracter in getting to the heart of our career compass point, of following our passion. We wish to ensure that our personal finances are neither a distracter from nor a blocker to our dreams.

Early in a career it seems so difficult to separate the role and its reward. Who hasn't (I know I have) taken a job or switched their career, just for the money? Few of us – certainly in the early part of our careers – can afford (literally) to be laid back about our earnings. After all, there are rents/mortgages to be paid, babies to be fed and perhaps well-earned holidays to be taken.

This early inability to separate what we do from what we earn can set a trend for the future: rather than a career, we are simply seeking a revenue stream. Rather than what we do being a route to defining who we are and who we become, our career simply becomes a measure of status. We shall ultimately see that the power in getting the balance and direction we want, and consequently setting our LifeCompass correctly, comes from separating these two factors: career (or, as we have seen, 'dharma') and finance (or, as we shall see, 'affluence') and considering them separately before we reconnect them. But before we move on, perhaps we should just ask a more fundamental question – does it really matter? Why not just do it for the money? And, to be honest, why not for the more money the better, then enjoy it all at some later stage?

This is not necessarily a ridiculous strategy. However, one difficulty comes when we finally catch up with the fact that money is actually rather a poor long-term motivator. It can't actually get you out of bed in the morning or more precisely it can't get you out of bed in the morning feeling life is fantastic if it is the only incentive you have. So to try and overcome the problem, we seek some kind of change: often more of something, such as more responsibility and often, of course, more money, believing that will do the trick. But it won't; eventually the effort of overcoming a job we simply don't enjoy is just too much. Then we either get the message or we have a crisis. If you're having a crisis, then that's maybe why you are reading this book. It will help.

The message is of course, seek, follow, chase your dharma, the revenue will follow. Really? Is that just a slick, new age sound bite? No, it's sound commercial sense. Do what you love and you'll do what you are good at; do what you are good at and you'll do it well; you'll do a good job; you'll be well paid; you'll be asked back and/or promoted … The essential point is that we put the emphasis on doing what we are good at, what we enjoy, what gives us passion. When we consider career and the associated financial reward separately, we give ourselves the chance to consider what to do and in fact who we want to be, rather than simply making a decision because of financial reasons.

But, hang on. Are you saying that you would actually like to be very wealthy? Well, don't be concerned. Nothing in the above negates that concept. In fact if you really want to be very wealthy, then release your talents. That is, of course, what we are talking about here.

We're going to assume that you have already done some work on the career compass point and feel you can see how you can make progress or are at least pretty happy with the way your career is going. It's now those wretched finances which irritate you. Let's do some work. Our goal in this section is firstly to de-emphasize finance as the number one motivator and make it simply a reward, a personal measure. Secondly, it is to sort out the practical aspect of managing finances: much of the focus on finances is because they are in such poor order. Let's start.

Actions

Take a moment to calibrate your current personal financial state on a scale of one to ten. If you are in a close relationship with someone and share much of your finances with him or her, it will be important that at some stage you have such a discussion with that person. However, at the moment just take your view. How does the scale work? Well, it's important to not get bogged down in the details of an exact scale. Here are some guidelines to the basic calibration.

Calibration 10

Calibration 10 equates to your financial state being excellent; there is little more you can do apart from regular monitoring of the situation. You know exactly what comes in and what goes out. Either you are currently financially independent (that is, you need never work again) or you know exactly (to the month and/or year) when you'll be financially independent and you're happy with that date. You know what you are currently worth financially. You're entirely financially knowledgeable yourself or you have good advisors and trust them. There is little more you could do at this stage apart from firstly continuing to be aware of market conditions and financial regulations and secondly continuing to review. Financial independence, as we mentioned, means that you would never need to work again. That doesn't mean that you wouldn't work, of course. If you are following your dharma, your life purpose (see Compass Point 1) then you would probably thrive on your work. The key indicators for calibration 10 are:

- *Your personal financial account is fully in control:*
  - *You know exactly what comes in and goes out.*

  - *Your account(s) are optimized for minimum account charges and best interest rates.*
  - *You are never overdrawn unless this is planned and optimized.*
  - *You have no loans unless they are deliberate strategies working for you; the most obvious example is a mortgage.*
- *You know your personal financial worth:*
  - *You have a personal balance sheet; that is, you have a simple calculation of your current assets less your current liabilities.*
  - *You aim to increase that by a certain percentage each year.*
- *The sum of money that you have projected for your financial independence meets your requirements. If you are currently financially independent, then you know that your long-term projections are sustainable.*

Mini case study

Although Sara knew there was plenty of work she had to do on the bigger perspectives of her compass, she certainly rated herself a clear ten for her personal finances. She put this down to early good advice from her father. She had always been a saver as a child and when she started work she had shifted that to becoming an investor. She would not tolerate debt unless there was a good longer-term reason, for example a mortgage. But even there she made the biggest repayments she could and spare cash went to reducing the capital she owed. She was 27 and had set a financial independence day of her fortieth birthday. She was on plan for that and in fact she would be able to achieve it on her thirty-seventh birthday. She had kept her personal balance sheet for the last ten years and that was her most fundamental tool in keeping things under control. She did have one adviser; it had taken a long time to find someone she trusted and she had read widely to understand as much she could. Having control of her finances had made her more relaxed about key career decisions. She always found it amusing that her friends thought she was 'boring' about her finances: she personally found her friends were actually more boring, being so limited in scope with what they could do. One thing her father had stressed was that good money management did not mean you stopped enjoying life: because of good money management you were able to enjoy life more. She was able to purchase the car she wanted. She was able to buy the flat she wanted. It gave her choice.

Calibration 5

At calibration 5 your finances are broadly understood. You know your ingoings and outgoings, although to be honest there could be a little more detail and you are aware there are some (relatively) small amounts of money that you are not tracking: what comes in and what goes out never seems to quite add up and balance. But you are concerned that you don't have a financial independence day in mind: you aren't that keen on current government plans to have you still working at 70. You are also worried that you don't understand a lot of financial terminology. The key indicators for calibration 5 are:

- *Account control a little 'fuzzy':*
  - *The account is not optimized; you waste money, perhaps by things such as late payments.*
  - *You don't have a clear document which states exactly what is going in and out.*
- *Financial independence day is not known, even approximately.*
- *You have a poor understanding of financial terms such as debt, cash flow, personal balance sheet.*

Mini case study

Andrew felt really frustrated by his personal finances; it wasn't as if he wasn't interested, but he just didn't seem to be able to get some kind of control mechanism. He had a horrid feeling that debt was costing him a lot of money, but at the moment he didn't have the foggiest idea just how much. He would take his girlfriend out on her birthday and pay the bill confidently with a credit card, but at the end of the month he would realize that, once again, he hadn't taken the extra expense into account and so the debt on his card would rise. He had a vague intention of clearing his debt as soon as he could but no real plan. He gave himself a rating of five. He knew he needed to do work and he was keen to do so. But where to start? So many newspaper articles on managing your finances seemed so general and books on the subject were too complicated. For him, anyway.

Calibration 0

At calibration 0 your finances are in a very poor state. You're regularly overdrawn; you don't know what comes in or out. As for financial planning: well! You realize that the thought of 'managing your finances' is an alien one. The key indicators for calibration 0 are:

- *You receive continuous financial shocks and dread any communication from the bank.*
- *You have no long-term financial planning.*

Mini case study

This was Lucy's nightmare: her finances. She had absolutely no strategy and loved to live day to day. Once it had seemed amusing, but unfortunately this was no longer so. She gave herself a rating of two. It had all started the day she arrived at university. She had never seen anything like it: an intense desire, it seemed, by everyone, to get wasted. She had never spent so much money on alcohol in one week and it had simply not stopped. Everything: fun, friendship, having a good time, seemed to revolve around money. And you'd have thought she could have caught up in the vacation with some serious earning through vacation jobs, but some of her friends decided to go travelling and it was too good an opportunity to miss …

Back to you. Now write down three actions you could take immediately, depending on your current calibration, which would begin to close the gap between where you are and where you would like to be.

For example, if your current calibration is 0 and you'd like it to become calibration 2:

Start recording what comes in and what goes out and to where. Get a notebook. And however well or badly you do it initially, keep at it. This is an absolute example of where knowledge is power. Don't give up when you feel that you have had a poor day and are a little embarrassed about recording the figures. Then cut up one credit card: start with the one with the highest interest rate (you don't know? Well, find out! Once again, knowledge is power), not necessarily the one with the highest outstanding amount. Finally, start saving £5 a month: this is as much for the ritual, for the shift of becoming a saver rather than a spender.

At calibration 5:

Cut up a couple more credit cards. If you have a string of them, now would be a good time to decide what uses they all have. Why do you have so many? If you are robbing one to pay the other that is a poor reason. If one has a design you like, that is as bad reason as using one that gives you loyalty points. Why have more than one card? Perhaps in order to maximize your free credit period, or so that you can distinguish work and personal finances or personal and joint accounts. Be sure you have a really good reason.

Establish your budgeting process. There's more information on this later, but essentially decide how you will decide. How will you know how much money you will allow yourself for your holidays? For your clothes? For clubbing?

Buy a book and build your financial literacy. There are many excellent ones; visit your local bookshop and flick through a selection. Choose one whose style you enjoy. Make the purchase: I'd encourage you not to rely on a library book because you need to read and re-read it and mark it up. You can also calculate when you can afford to retire!

If your current calibration is 9:

Why aren't you a ten? Check the advice you receive. Are all your advisers trusted and validated? Have you double-checked their figures? You don't know how? What would it take for you to reach their level of expertise? You could, at least, get another adviser to check their figures. How independent are your advisers? You can also improve your savings (both amounts and schemes). Presumably this would take you up to that top calibration. You can also start a virtual stock portfolio and learn more about the stock market.

Now write down some longer-term actions, for example: calibration 0: read a financial advice book; calibration 7: set up and practise with a dummy stock market portfolio.

Insights

Revitalize the basics of good financial management. Every one of the following points should be common sense for you. But do remember that common sense is not necessarily common practice.

Key 1

Spend less than you earn and save the rest. If you do nothing else, ensure this becomes your personal financial mantra. You may well have noticed that however much you earn, you simply seem to spend more. That the promotion you received and the associated salary increase, far from solving your current debt problems as you had hoped it might, actually made them worse. That's because the imagination takes off when we think we have more money to spend. Break that pattern. Know how much you earn, exactly. Exactly. Know how much you have to spend, exactly. Exactly. Ensure the former is greater than the latter. Year on year, strive to save a greater percentage of your overall budget. This is not being a control freak. This is not removing the spontaneity in your life. The opportunity to have money, to not be in debt, allows us all to create and have more spontaneity.

Key 2

Create a simple system of 'jars'. This is a strategy borrowed from the great financial planners of the 1950s. A jar is simply a budgeted allocation of money. Thus you need a jar for your food spend and a jar for your entertainment spend and a jar for your mortgage, etc. The more specific you make the jar, the more control you will find that you have. Of course I don't suggest that you literally keep a selection of jam jars on your mantlepiece – although if you are really bad at managing your finances then this might be a solution! You can just keep a notebook (paper or electronic), for instance, with a few pages for each category of expense with a budget allocated for that month. At the end of the month go through the cheques written and your credit card statements and note which category of spending each amount comes from. It will soon become clear, for example, if you are allocating £100 to clothes but spending £150. Then you have a choice. Spend less on clothes, cut down elsewhere or earn more. Or some combination of the three. Your current approach is not sustainable. Brainstorm the jars that you need. Try these suggestions as a starter.

Food and household shopping

This allocation is for the regular family spend on food and household needs. Start recording a few shopping trips (jot down a list beforehand and hang onto it for later review): what do you spend your money on at the supermarket? Perhaps decide to devote one of your shopping trips (say an online one) each week to basics only: bread, cereals, etc. This is often an area where a little focus can give some good savings; many of the items can be found at lower prices. Do everything you can here to get the costs down without compromising significantly on quality: remember, what's the point if the teabags are 15% cheaper but taste disgusting, or the instant coffee needs twice as much to taste of anything? However, many cleaning materials are perfectly adequate in unbranded forms. Tips for keeping costs down and quality up are:

- *Shop with a prepared list; decide balanced meals for the week ahead. Keep your lists on your computer and print them out when you go.*
- *Start noticing what you buy. The process of simply giving attention to your shopping will bring down your spending. Refocus on what something costs.*

Test yourself and/or your partner. Be surprised how expensive some of those impulse purchases are.

- *Shop online; save time. Yes it may cost a little extra, but – and an important point here – begin to think about your own time. What value do you put on that? If a £5 delivery charge gets you two hours of extra time (the commute plus the actual shop), isn't that worth a lot? Shopping online has many advantages. It eliminates much impulse purchase shopping, websites allow easy comparison shopping once you understand them and it allows basics and necessities to be bought easily so you can have fun with the variable parts of the list.*
- *Consider reducing and/or eliminating alcohol during the week. For two reasons: the first one is a chance to link this compass point to your mind/body compass point; the second is, of course, a chance to make some significant savings. One bottle of wine per night, say £5. Per week, say £25. Say £100 a month, say £1000 a year – never mind the chance you've given your liver to recover.*

Entertainment

This allocation is concerned with going out, cooking special meals. Set up good habits. What do you enjoy doing? Clubbing? Cinema? Theatre? Entertaining friends? Decide your budget and stick to it; it'll make you more discerning. It'll encourage you to think of ways to have fun without spending money: this in itself is a fantastic mindset to adopt. It'll ensure you do value the times you do spend out at the theatre or wherever.

Alcohol

This category can be an expensive one and is certainly worth separating from entertainment and/or the food and household spend as it often grows into a significant amount of money. Agree to track your alcohol spend for a month. Be shocked! And do note that it'll be a whole lot bigger over Christmas, New Year and any family celebration period.

Holiday

Separate weekend breaks and short breaks from your main family holiday. Keep track especially of all that money you spend on 'stress busters'. This is particularly important if you are wondering where all your double-income money is going. More on this point later, but something to begin to think about now: did you realize that although you have the benefit of two incomes, the simple fact that you are both working will of course incur associated costs, many of which are far from insignificant? For example, those stress busters, dry cleaning, child care, two smart and/or reliable cars, expensive ready-meal costs …

Insurance

A tricky one. The insurance industry is very good at getting us to feel we should insure everything that moves. But certainly check that you have got the essentials such as life insurance, house contents insurance. This is one to think laterally on, perhaps, especially if you are basically in good health and are doing everything you can to proactively look after yourself. Perhaps it isn't necessary for you to sign up for expensive health insurance but simply put a fixed amount aside instead to pay for any emergency operation privately should you need and choose to do so. You may not need to consider this if you are in a company scheme, but it may be helpful once you retire.

Personal investment

Decide to spend 2% of your overall income on investing in you: in your brain. Very few of us do this. In fact most people invest more money in their car than they do in their brain. Invest in books, courses, in fact anything to make you more effective.

Children

The question of pocket money, allowance. Define these for the children. Try and come up with some logic for increases that are age or need related. Be very careful about being driven by the '… but X has got one' line.

Christmas

This is a huge expense for most families and can easily blow a huge hole in the budget. Agree what you want to do. This raises a bigger issue, but it might spur a return to the concept of a simple Christmas.

Presents

Which are the regular birthdays, the anniversaries which need to be celebrated? Predetermine the money to be put aside.

Personal allowance

Decide your personal allowance, that is one for non-measurable expenses. If you have a shared account, make sure you each have an agreed personal allowance.

House

Invest in your property. This not only avoids shocks in the future, it also ensures that when you come to sell you can redeem the full value.

Rainy day

Establish an easily accessible emergency fund for the odd crisis that you haven't budgeted for elsewhere. Do ensure that it is infrequently raided. If it is being used a lot it probably means another jar is insufficient or even that there is a specific jar that is missing.

Save

This category is fundamental for your future, of course. Just check that this doesn't become a black hole for when all your other budgets fail. Ensure you are saving specifically for, firstly, retirement (that is the day at which you no longer wish to be dependent upon external income); secondly, for emergencies and thirdly for specific projects such as extending the house.

Once you have a definitive list of your jars, then you need to allocate a budget against each one. Play with and adjust these until the budget meets your needs. Sometimes it can be better to decide a percentage budget which you wish to spend. This can be revealing if you discover you are spending 25% of your income on entertainment. If you are familiar with using a spreadsheet, then it can allow you to play with these figures very easily.

Total your figures. If they come to more than you are earning then you need to reduce them or earn more. The latter is a longer-term aim and needs to be carefully considered so that it doesn't distract you from your main career goal. The former is the one to work on first.

When you review your personal compass each month, set a personal goal to slowly but surely improve your calibration.

Advanced insights

We have the basic insights addressed: now we need to look at the more advanced ones. Some of these are more philosophical and will need considerable thought on your part, but equally these will be the areas which will cause you the greatest impact.

Become aware of the double-income myth

Consider the following situation: a long-term, committed relationship, both partners with interesting yet demanding careers. Children arrive on the scene. Should both of them remain working? This will, of course, be for the couple themselves to consider. And the points they might consider are:

- *The money that is generated through one/both working.*
- *The satisfaction/growth/career development that is provided by one/both working.*
- *The benefits for the child/children of one/both working.*
- *The overall benefits to the family of one/both working.*

As you can see, the potential reasons are various and, as always, are rarely separated but are strongly interconnected. I'm not going to debate the parenting pros and cons of both partners working but simply look at the financial aspects. This is not a statement about whether it is better or worse to take a certain route, but if you do feel that you must both work for the money then you do need to check that you will actually be financially better off if you do. It may not be the case.

Sometimes surprisingly – considering the input that has to be made, especially when stress, etc. is taken into account – the return is not necessarily that attractive. This can help to give you more confidence if your preferred route would be for one of you to stay at home and look after the children. Let's take a quick look at this. When you are both earning, these things need to be considered:

- *Tax: possible higher income tax because of overall higher income.*
- *Clothing and appearance: there will be a consequential extra spend on clothes in order to maintain a smart appearance.*
- *Transport: it may be that an extra car will be needed or possibly a more reliable car. Many families even introduce a third car for the nanny.*
- *Childcare: the biggest and most probable expense is childcare, either at a day nursery or possibly with a live-in au pair. Sometimes people manage to make arrangements with their parents; this can have a downside, such as restricted ability to move or more stressful relationships with parents or in-laws.*
- *Stress management and/or rewards: the need for regular stress-busters.*
- *Financial management: the need for an external adviser to manage finances.*

This is such a complex topic that I've revisited it briefly later, after the questions and answers section.

The cost of a job you are not enjoying

Think about this. Be aware that when we are not enjoying a job then we tend to compensate through many different factors, many of which cost money and continue the need for a high-earning job. Ironically, when we switch to one which we enjoy more fully, even if it is lower paid, we find that many costs fall away. Notice that when you are enjoying your job and it is fulfilling you, then your expenses are often very modest. But with a job which you don't enjoy the stress-related and job-caused expenses can rocket.

Address your limiting belief(s)

Many individuals simply do not believe that they can gain control of their finances, let alone begin to develop financial independence. Remember that your beliefs drive your behaviour and your behaviour drives your results. Beliefs will get you the results that you think you deserve. Here are some empowering beliefs to try out:

- *I can get my finances under my control. Step by step, just ten minutes a day. Record your expenses in a notebook, collate those credit card vouchers. By control I mean simply what comes in and what goes out. Start making financial decisions, conscious ones.*
- *I can break the equivalence between spending and happiness. When 'retail therapy' has moved beyond an amusing label and become an apparently serious way of thinking you know it's time to take action. And, yes, your upbringing may have done all kinds of odd things to the way you view money, but now is a time to move on from that. You can only analyze the past, but you can design the future. Take that option. Decide to identify low cost and free ways to have a good time to sit alongside the ones which take up a lot of money.*
- *I can make financial independence an option for me. I can bring the date forward and I can increase the amount I have to play with. Here's the way.*
  - *Stage 1: When do you want it? By when would you like to be financially independent?*
  - *Stage 2: How much do you want?*
  - *Stage 3: Integrate this with dharma thinking.*
  - *Stage 4: Ask yourself clearly why you want it. Is it so that you have the ultimate choice over any request? Is it so that you feel your status would be raised? Is it simply an exciting goal? After all, one reason many people wish for financial independence is the freedom to 'escape', but if what you are doing is what you truly love, do you need to escape?*
- *I can learn to focus more on true affluence rather than simple wealth. I can learn to appreciate relationships, time, walks, a great play …*
- *We can live as well if not better with just one income rather than two. We are, after all, two bright, creative people who have the joy of a new baby on the way. We can do it.*
- *I can get my employers to support my job-sharing and/or part-time working wishes. I simply need to argue my case better than I have ever done before. I*

need to improve my assertiveness skills.

- *I will break the social conditioning which tells me that I must do this and I must have this sofa and this music, and that my children are not loved unless I can buy them … I will break that and I will do it now.*
- *I will raise the children so that they understand the often relentless, seductive force of peer pressure. I will encourage then to think for themselves and not necessarily follow the crowd.*

Decide now to realize that if this compass point is important for you, then there is nothing to stop you achieving management of your finances very quickly and, once you have achieved that, develop a plan for achieving independence. Don't be held back by a poor belief. You'll now have a good understanding of how limiting beliefs come about; one, of course, is a result of poor understanding. As we gain knowledge and financial literacy we will find that our beliefs will change.

There is often confusion between the two terms 'standard of living' and 'quality of life'

For many, these two terms seem to be equivalent. They are not, certainly in the longer term. By 'standard of living' I mean level of possessions, from hot and cold running water to central heating, from juicer to television to timeshare in Morocco to designer clothes. This list is a list of things. We want them because of what they give us. And we hope that is 'quality of life'. By quality of life I mean living the life you want to live: fun, happiness, enjoyment. As you think about it, you will realize that they are not equivalent; one does not necessarily lead to the other. Interestingly, many people suddenly realize that their standard of living has become so high that it is reducing their quality of life; the pressure of maintaining that level of possessions means they have little time to enjoy them or be themselves or do the simple things in life. Chase quality of life not standard of living; you are then likely to hit the correct threshold of desire. Alternatively, if it helps

when you are building your wish list of stuff, add to it some intangibles, particularly time and relationships.

There can be a concern between worry over control and management

They are different. Don't worry, this process and way of thinking won't turn you into a control freak. It'll simply give you more options. When we manage something, it doesn't need to control us: it simply allows us to manage our life. Management is not about restriction. It's actually about freedom of choice, about options.

The overall concept of affluence

Begin to start thinking about this. We may not always be financially well off but we can be affluent in terms of rich relationships, health, etc. True wealth for many comes when we stop thinking purely about cash or stock or property values but in terms of the intangibles we have: the love of our children, going on a beautiful walk, the magic of a medieval building, a marvellous piece of theatre, helping another individual, baking a birthday cake for a special person. Unfortunately sometimes when we become too involved in this aspect of financial planning we actually damage much of what would give us true affluence. Begin this process by doing a stream-of-consciousness gratitude list. Simply jot down everything for which you are grateful. How about these:

- *Family/friends.*
- *Partner/spouse.*
- *Health.*
- *House.*
- *Freedom.*
- *Great literature.*
- *Training.*
- *Skill development.*
- *Cooking a great meal.*
- *Music.*

Money and personal worth

Decide now not to equate your personal worth with your level of earnings. Equate it with you and your purpose, you and your overall compass. Move beyond the label of your job title, your grade on the company scheme, the car you are allowed to have and whether you are allowed to use economy or club class when flying to the States.

Choice

Finally, choice. In the end few of us are truly motivated by money (and if you doubt that let me assure you that most of the senior-level coaching that I do revolves around this issue: 'I have everything and yet nothing'). Money is a tool. Money gives us choice. Money (itself) does not give us happiness. And you may want to read that last sentence one more time.

Mini case study: Andrew

Remember Andrew, who gave himself a calibration of five? His first challenge was that he had no idea what state his finances were in, apart from the fact that he earned a reasonable salary but was always struggling and that he seemed to be paying a lot of interest on his debt. Here's what he did:

- *Month 1. He decided this would be would be 'lock down' month. He would go into survival mode and only spend the minimum: rent and food was essentially it. Nothing on clothes or going out. It was tough but revealing. He recorded it all in his notebook: both the actual figures but also where he had been tempted into to spending money. He realized that there was a lot of psychology in this money business for him. His friends thought he was a bit odd being so draconian, but he felt zero tolerance was the only way as far as he was concerned.*
- *Month 2. He created a budget as a result of his research. He made a commitment that he would only spend if it came out of his budget. The budget totals matched his income and he deliberately built in savings and a special category for paying off his debt. Although initially limiting, managing his finances rather than his finances managing him felt good.*

- *Month 3. Debt was already dropping rapidly. He cut up all his credit cards, bar two: one for work and one for pleasure. His plan was to pay these off in full each month.*
- *Month 4. He switched his mortgage to a better deal, revamped his pension, paid off a car loan.*
- *Month 5. He was where he wanted to be. He had the best mortgage for him, his pension was sorted, he had no debt bar his mortgage and he had budgeted his spending. He also had a lot less stress.*

Mini case study: Lucy

Lucy had given herself a calibration of two and was really depressed about her situation. She hated the fact that any pleasurable spending was immediately followed by the stress, pain and anguish of having to sort out her debt, grovel to bank managers and rob one credit card to pay another. She'd made no impact on repaying her student loan and was no nearer to making any savings towards a house.

Following a workshop, Lucy realized she would need to change her state and get herself into one where she was inclined to take action. This she did: better sleep, better diet, bit more exercise. After that it was easy. She then listed all the fun things she could do without spending money and created some envelopes (her jars) which held the money that she would allow herself to spend.

Questions and answers

I sense this question is another one of those 'can I really' ones. Anyway, I'm 23; can I really expect financial independence before I am, say, 60/65 and even then won't it be at a very modest level?

You can. But first you must put aside your limiting belief which says that financial independence is beyond you or is not a right of yours. Secondly you must calibrate what you want from financial independence. Will a million be enough? Or five million or more? And when? Equally, ask yourself why you wish for financial independence. Is it simply because you wish to do something else? In which case, what do you need to do to be able to do that now? Or is it that you wish for security? In that case, what would give you security now?

I'm just dreadful with money, especially credit cards. What are some practical tips?

Be careful with a label such as 'I'm just dreadful with credit cards'. That is your past experience: it is a label which you are giving yourself which does not help; in fact it may well hinder you. Importantly, it need not be your future experience. How about if you decided 'I'm getting better with credit cards'? On practical steps, your first is to detail your credit cards: name, amount due and rate of interest. Start paying them off in order of highest rate first. Cut up one card. For your weekly purchases – food, entertainment, etc. – use cash.

I do like the idea of dharma and I do believe in it, but to really 'follow your dharma' and believe the money will come in … is this just new age fantasy?

No. Plenty of people are following their dharma already, from traffic wardens to science teachers, from cooks to surgeons. The important question is: what is your dharma, what is it that gives you the buzz you need? And how can you start slowly but surely working towards it? Revisit Compass Point 1.

Double income, double bind?

As I noted earlier, this is a challenging topic on which to clarify our thinking. It can be laden with history (men being breadwinners), politics, feminism (women have a fundamental right to work), confusion (will I be bored if I don't work?), consumerism (which lifestyle are you adopting by working/not working?), status (who wants to say 'I stay at home and look after the kids'?). Whatever, I did promise to come back to it, and it is important to do so as this area will make a huge impact on our ability to resolve our finance compass point if we are in this situation.

Put aside those loaded points initially and let's not even think about the money aspect. Come at it from the aspect of your relationship and what you want from it. What do you really want? What do you want for each other? What is your joint vision? If children are part of that vision, then what do you wish for them? If you haven't done this, if you have low clarity on this aspect, then now would be a very good time to address the idea.

Remind yourself that dharma ultimately allows yourself to express yourself, to be true to yourself. It allows you to express, to contribute, to grow. Our dharma is not purely about revenue stream (that is a benefit, of course) nor is it about a label ('I am an account manager for …').

You can now link that with a second stage which is the quality of life/standard of living discussion. You may love your dharma – but do you want to do it all the time? If you are developing your dharma, maybe you could be doing something else part-time.

And then move to a third stage – if you have children or are planning to have children, how do you want them to be brought up? What values are important, how will you model those and what skills will you need? How will you ensure confidence? If you talk long and deeply to your partner you may find that you want to make a greater commitment to your children, and that one of you wishes to look after them full time.

Now for stage four – can you afford to do that?

I hope through our discussions you have realized that you can:

- *Think bigger picture. Money truly isn't everything. Focus on dharma, relationships and support for the children.*
- *Reinforce the difference: standard of living/quality of life.*
- *Realize the associated costs of a double income.*
- *Realize the damaging mindset of 'keeping up with the Joneses'.*
- *Think outside the box.*

Bonus section

Bonus: The psychology of money

Let's not leave finance until we have recognized and admitted to ourselves that money is, of course, more complicated than being just a medium for transactions. Being a medium for transactions it also becomes:

- *A measure of worth: decide that money won't measure your worth.*
- *A hold over somebody: decide that it won't have a hold over you.*
- *A measure of success: decide that money will only be an incidental measure of success for you.*
- *A giver of security: decide that it will not be your measure of security.*
- *A giver of freedom: decide that you will choose freedom.*

Summary

The finance compass point is concerned – at the most fundamental level – with addressing finances so that they are neither a distracter nor a cause of unnecessary anxiety. At higher levels this compass point is concerned with recognizing that we can shift our thinking towards true affluence, the important things in life and financial independence. Our finances are simply a support to whatever is most important in life.

Chapter 6

Compass Point 4: Relationships

Life is full of relationships: with our friends, our colleagues and our families. Some of these are short term: a colleague with whom we work briefly on a virtual team project. Some, such as with a partner, may well last a lifetime. We are always in a cluster of ever-shifting external relationships. Plus, of course, that ever-nagging internal relationship: our relationship with ourselves.

Few of us can claim that all of the relationships in our life, our most intimate, those with our friends and those in our working lives, are always as we would like them to be. They can bring us joy, they can bring us misery and they can be just OK; they are rarely static. They ebb and flow. Consider three relationships in your life: one most personal, one a child or parent, and one a business relationship. Take a moment and ask yourself, for each one, what would be the one thing you could do to make that relationship even better than it is at the moment. Take a minute to consider this and jot down your thoughts. You may have a feeling of irritation as you think that the other person should be doing this exercise as it's their fault that the relationship isn't as it should be. Or perhaps you have a feeling of despair as you wonder whether the relationship will ever work. Leave those feelings aside for the moment. And even if you feel that the relationship is perfect, simply, for the moment, jot down a thought, an action. Finally, what might improve your relationship with yourself? When do you feel you excel? When do you let yourself down?

Insights

Here are a few insights which may help you with the relationships you would like to improve, plus some practical ideas for the relationship you would like to create. Remember that it's much harder to have a complete relationship with one person than superficial relationships with many. Decide the relationships which are very important to you. Look after them. Accept those that you cannot spend as much time with as you would like. It is easy to be torn apart and 'spoil' the most significant relationships in addition to damaging your relationship with yourself. And, by the way, I certainly won't be suggesting that you have to continue in all relationships: some simply come to an end. It may help, initially, to have a simple structure for the way we look at relationships. We'll first look at the Five As, and then at the importance of not waiting.

The Five As of relationships

The first A: Attention

A relationship needs attention for it to grow and develop. Simply by giving those three relationships I asked you to consider earlier some thought, time and attention, I'm sure you have already realized a few ways to make them even better. When with someone, whether it's in a formal setting (perhaps a manager or team colleague) or an informal one (a child), always give them 100% attention. Turn to face them, really tune into what they are saying. Look into their faces and put aside your other concerns temporarily in personal relationships. In business relationships, turn away from that spreadsheet: listen, take notes, whatever would be appropriate. With children, perhaps slow down a little and get down to their level. The simplest things become so much easier once we recognize the importance of attention. Let's take some examples; firstly, in business.

Learn names. When you meet someone, put aside your frustration with the journey, your worry about whether you'll remember everything you wish to say and instead hear the person's name, use it and learn it. This forces you to start your connection with them. This is not simply about being respectful and showing someone that you know their name, but the art of giving that focus causes you to engage more fully with the meeting. It is such a simple touch and yet is forgotten by most.

Don't lose the plot. So much of business is about relationships and so much of the art of building a relationship is about attention. For example, the customer experience is truly about creating small nuances of interaction. Instead we often insist on measuring hard quantitative data, such as the length of call time, simply because it's measurable. Consequently we damage the factor we are trying to protect (in that specific example, overly focusing on reducing average call time when a badly handled call, short or long, will just come back to bite you).

Attend to team development, particularly the development of a high-performing team. How can you build a high-performance team without attention? Some high-performance managers believe that they can. Guess what? They can't. Each person in that team must have time spent with them, to help them progress and to focus on their concerns.

Mini case study

Steve was a good technician. He had worked his way up through hotline support and was now running his first team. His first session of 360 degree feedback was a shock, though. He had expected to get a straightforward message that he, Steve, was a good manager, although perhaps not yet a dynamic one. Instead he was berated consistently for his lack of interest in people as individuals. After the shock, and his initial defensiveness, Steve read his notes on the Five As again and decided to give more attention to each person in the team. He spent just a little more time with them as individuals; he talked less and just listened. He talked less and just encouraged. He talked less and just focused on what was working well and on giving praise. It worked wonders: not only did productivity soar, he enjoyed the process and his next review session was a very positive one.

Now let's look at examples in personal life.

Attend to your relationship with your children. Have you been at one of those dinner parties where there are endless arguments about quality time or quantity time? As so often with poor thinking, it's become an unnecessarily polarized discussion. Of course it cannot be either/or, it has to be both. A useful term to express this is 'engagement time', time when you are there for your child. Not just physically, but also mentally. In this 24/7 world, it's not just our physical presence, it's our mental one too. When you are with your child, are you genuinely there? Or are you actually worrying about when you can start working on your email or how soon you can get them off to bed? Or whether you could keep them quiet with their third video of the day?

Attend to your relationship with your partner. When you are in a conversation, ensure that you are giving it 100% attention. This will ensure that whatever you are discussing will be dealt with more effectively and that your relationship will continue to improve. Work out what attention means for your partner. Maybe they don't want that much time; maybe simply knowing that you are there for them may be enough.

In both business and personal relationships it is no sign of weakness to actually ask the people who work for you – or those in your personal life – what the best way is for you to work with them. In your personal life, try asking 'what's the best way for me to love you?'. Are these crazy, artificial questions? Perhaps, if your relationship – business or personal – is currently perfect. But if not, give it a go. You may be surprised at the small, irritating things that come in the way. Your partner is grumpy and you try all kinds of things but in the end, after a heated discussion, you find that it is all to do with the total mess which you regularly leave in the kitchen after cooking. Or your relationship eases considerably when you both agree that you'll take a bit of time out after a hard week's work before starting discussions about the kids, the weekend, the shopping and the respective problems you are both having with your employers.

Let's summarize attention by returning to the perennial argument over quantity time or quality time. Quality time is the focus for business. Quantity time is the focus for our personal life; it is where the magic moments happen, where kids say great things, where they share their insights. In the business/working environment, it is increasingly difficult to find quantity time. And that perhaps does not matter too much; go for quality time. Raise your standards, do an outstanding job. It is our personal lives which are so much more unpredictable and which deserve spontaneous, creative time. Simply allow time to be, available time. Above all, don't create more working time by pinching it from personal time.

Mini case study

Robert was a single parent. He worked for four days a week and was constantly pulled in all directions with the demands of his job and trying to bring up his two young children after the death of their mother. He had been determined to try and do things well in the house: to keep it clean, stay away from junk food, ensure the children kept up with their activities and above all ensure that he was the main role model: certainly not using a child minder or even the grandparents, however wonderful they might be. But he did realize that, as far as any decent engagement time went – for reading stories, for drawing, for whatever – he was forever saying 'later'. Attending a workshop reminded him to give real attention to his children. Although he was not exactly flush with money he decided to 'outsource' the cleaning. That immediately gave him time and conserved some of his energy. He chatted to the children and drew up a chart which he stuck on the playroom wall. This told them their various activities such as swimming and also times when he would definitely be available for play and a couple of times when he wouldn't. It all started working a lot, lot better.

The second A: Awareness of difference

Be aware of differences between you and another. We are all unique. Apart from obvious cosmetic changes and differences of sex and culture, there will be differences such as these: how you like to discuss something; do you like to go straight in or do you prefer to warm up, how you decide what is important to you, what your beliefs are (that everyone has a right to a university education, for example, or that men and women are fundamentally the same) and your values (like integrity: whether you would lie to your children about your student excesses). Where did all these come from? Do they work for you? How about some other fundamental ones? In business, what do we mean by integrity? By loyalty, by success? In our personal lives, again what do we mean by loyalty? Not so sure about those? Try these:

In business: how do you think the people you lead and work with would respond to these queries if you were to ask the question of each and every one of them?

- *When do you feel I am appropriately leading you/communicating with you?*
- *How do you like to be praised?*
- *How do you like to be kept informed?*
- *What does 'accurate' mean to you?*

In your personal life, at an appropriate time, how about asking your partner for his/her views on:

- *How you want to educate the kids?*
- *What should we save for?*
- *What is your dream house?*
- *How would you like to celebrate your birthday?*
- *What is loyalty to each other?*

Consider speed of thinking. Some of us have immediate thoughts, some of us need to mull things over for a while; think about the relationship with time. Some of us like order and structure; some of us like to be a bit more open-ended.

Realize that, thank goodness, your life partner, your business colleague, your child is very different from you. So don't expect them to have the same views as you, or the same approach as you or believe the same things. And consider accepting: that is OK. Ironically, in business we often prize difference highly when it's known as creativity, but at other times we can resent it. By the way, this is not excusing poor behaviour. Someone who regularly turns up late to a meeting is being rude. Someone who is aggressive is being rude. These examples are not about difference, they're about poor behaviour.

A very powerful 'vocabulary for difference' is the Myers Briggs Type Indicator (MBTI). This introduces a more formal language for how we are each different. And although all indicators, by definition, will do an element of labelling, MBTI remains powerful but generic: it does not illustrate right or wrong but what is. Our 'is' is sometimes an asset and sometimes a liability. There are four scales in MBTI. Each scale addresses a different aspect of personality.

The first scale is the degree of introversion/extroversion. This is an indicator of how an individual is energized (note that this is different from the popular use of extroversion/introversion as simply a measure of sociability). Introverts are internally energized; they need down time and the ability to reflect and are sometimes accused of being quiet or overly reflective. Remember this is the way they 'are'. They can, of course, flex their behaviour but when they do it is more tiring. Extroverts, on the other hand, need discussion and action: they like to talk through their ideas. They are often told that they are too loud or inconsiderate. They can flex, too: reflect quietly for a while but, equally, that can be tiring for them. Think for a moment about how these fundamental differences might cause challenges in your relationships. Are you a bit fed up sometimes that your partner does not want to party all weekend? Maybe they are more of an introvert than you are. Or that one of your team colleagues always seems to need to talk through ideas? Maybe they are a little more extrovert than you are.

The second scale of potential fundamental difference is sensing/intuition. This scale is a measure of how we look at data, how we handle it. Some of us prefer the big picture (these are the so-called 'intuitors'), some prefer detail (the so-called 'sensors'). Do you sometimes just see the big picture possibilities and get frustrated when someone mentions the detail? Is the house 'just right' with loads of potential; why then does your partner see problems with wiring and draughty windows? Perhaps this is sensor–intuitor difference? Or are you frustrated that the key messages in the marketing presentation are all very big picture and that no one seems to be able to get down to the detail, which is crucially important for you?

The next scale, thinking/feeling, is a measure of how an individual makes a decision and is one which can cause a lot of challenges, especially in personal relationships. In addition to there being a fundamental difference in thinking, there is in addition also here an apparent sex bias. 'Thinkers' prefer to make their decisions in a Cartesian or Newtonian if–then kind of way. 'Feelers' prefer to use relevant values to decide how they will go about a decision.Seventy per cent of men are thinkers, seventy percent of women are feelers. Thinkers prefer systems, feelers are empathizers and they do not always see eye to eye! Maybe you are discussing money and one of you (the thinker) is logically arguing to save a certain amount every month. But perhaps your partner (the feeler) feels that it's better to save when the money is available and that this will work out more effectively in the long run anyway. Perhaps in the business environment, a feeler believes that an expenses claim is justified because the circumstances were unusual; perhaps a thinker manager believes that the claim must be disallowed whatever the circumstances.

The final scale is judging/perceiving. This concerns closure and degree of being 'sorted out'. Do you prefer to know exactly what you are going to do next? Then you are probably more judging (notice that is judging and not judgemental). Do you prefer some spontaneity? Does a detailed diary, with everything scheduled, bring you out in a cold sweat? Then maybe you are more of a perceiver.

Mini case study

Pam's introduction to MBTI and the whole concept of difference was a revelation. She had always seen herself as very accepting of big differences such as race or sex. But she realized she was actually very judging when it came down to minor differences in the work environment, such as the way an explanation should be given. She realized that what she was putting down to poor performance in one individual was probably simply an MBTI difference.

The third A: Appreciate

At home, at work, thank people for what they've done for you. Never assume. Focus on the positive and what is working well. The simplest builder of an excellent relationship is genuine appreciation and connection with the other person.

At work, thank for things like these:

- *Helping with a presentation.*
- *Making you feel welcome in a new team.*
- *Getting some informal but useful coaching.*
- *Giving guidance.*
- *Mentioning a possible career route.*

Return the compliment whenever you can. At work we know that the biggest single motivator is simply a genuine 'thank you'.

At home say thank you for these sorts of things:

- *Shopping.*
- *Cooking.*
- *Being there.*
- *Sex.*
- *Listening.*

In the home we know that what can lead to most stress is not feeling appreciated.

The fourth A: Affection

In personal relationships, be interested in what interests your friend, child or lover. Be careful about judging. Hug more often. Look into their eyes and get to really know them. Consider this in relation to awareness of difference. Be aware that we can show our affection in different ways; affection for some is being tidy or helping with the cooking. It may be always being there with a hug or being wickedly sexy, or remembering an important date. It may be several of these or none of these. It could be simply be being accepting of them when others haven't been. And who wants a relationship with a robot anyway?

The fifth A: Action

In any relationship, start: take action. Particularly when a relationship is not working. The biggest influencer of another's behaviour is your own. Put your ego aside. Start now. In business, ask the person concerned for a dedicated 15 minutes. Sit down with them, explain the issue. You'll be amazed at how often they agree they should have done something about it ages ago.

Mini case study

Colin was having such challenges with his new manager: it was really depressing him. It was the first time he had actually felt bullied in the whole of his career. He'd tried a variety of approaches including, he had to admit, simply sulking, but it didn't seem to be getting him anywhere. The breakthrough came when he decided that they had to talk; there was nothing to be lost. Once they did so Colin realized that it had all been the simplest of miscommunications. It really is true that in business there are very few real bastards; maybe one or two, but not many considering the huge number of people we come across in our working lives.

Don't wait

The Five As were our first important insight in this compass point. The second important insight clarifies the fifth A: action. Don't wait for 'them' before changing your behaviours. Start now and notice the benefits. Remember that most relationships are simply not at their best because we don't look after them. As I mentioned above there may be one or two real bastards, especially in the corporate world. However, let me assure you that they do not sleep well at night and that they're usually scared stiff. They are in a minority, however. Do what you can and don't spend unnecessary time with them. Be yourself, be warm to people. Encourage others to accept you as you are. Love the appropriate ones. See the magic it generates.

Now, what about you? Consider how the whole Five A structure can work very well for you.

Attention. Give yourself time and attention. What do you really love doing? When can you next do it? Take time out for yourself. Not just going shopping, but doing whatever is important for you. Reading: set aside an hour and explain to everyone in the family that it's your reading time and you don't want to be disturbed. Learn how to invest in yourself: what do you want to do? Make sure that every week you get some decent time to yourself.

Awareness. Yes, you are different from your colleagues. Some of them are noisy, some of them ... well, that doesn't mean you are not effective. Develop your self-awareness to new heights so that you can work with others and so that you can work to your natural strengths. Couple with that your ability to be curious; what is it like to think in that kind of way? What are the benefits, for example, of being a very detailed thinker?

Appreciation. What are you doing well? What changes have you made? Catch yourself doing things right. Don't beat yourself up: it's unlikely that you'll get everything perfectly right first time.

Affection. Allow yourself some TLC. Decide to invest in yourself.

Action. Start now!

Questions and answers

Are there people in business I won't be able to form practical working relationships with?

You can probably, by using these ideas, get a practical working relationship going with anyone. That does not mean they will be your best buddy and it does not mean all tensions in the relationship will disappear. But, more fundamentally, by using these ideas with everyone we will develop some excellent relationships.

I've got some people I deal with and they are simply aggressive.

Do you really need to work with them? If you do, then so be it. If not, try and stay out of their circle of control or their sphere of influence. If you do need to work with them, ensure you know the skills of assertiveness. Assertiveness is in essence remembering that an excellent relationship can only be formed when each side of the relationship treats the other side with respect. What do we really mean by respect? Respecting the other person's rights. Some rights are common to all such as the right to common courtesy, or to being able to express a view without guilt or cynicism, or feeling that doing so might damage our next review. Some are particular to a job, such as having the final decision on how to proceed with a deal.

I'm really on a roll with my personal development. But my partner is simply not interested. There's so much I'd like to do, particularly in our personal relationship area.

Stay loving. There are many reasons your partner may not be interested. They may be perfectly content or stressed or fearful of the change you will undertake, or maybe even suspicious. Stay loving, model excellent behaviours yourself and it will work out.

Actions

So, what actions will *you* take?

Bonus section

Bonus 1: Quantity and quality time

This is the endless debate. In the busy world in which we live and in which we often feel guilty about the time we are giving to a relationship, we talk endlessly about quantity and quality time. Let's return to the basics: what do we wish to achieve? In our working lives we are trying to meet an objective and it does not matter whether that working objective is to hit this quarter's sales figures or to create a TV script or produce four new watercolours for an exhibition. We must put the time in, develop our expertise and technique, and then produce the quality we seek. We will get what we want through the product of two factors: quantity time and quality time. However, for many of us, our emphasis needs to move to the quality time side of the equation. We are using the excuse of insufficient time, when the real issue is insufficient quality. Decide to schedule the time, raise your standards and give the task absolute focus.

In our personal relationships the degree of unknowns is much larger. What are we seeking? The time to enjoy the relationship, the time to build and develop the relationship, to have sufficient time together so that we avoid misunderstandings. This again is about quality time and quantity time. But interestingly, for the magic of personal relationships to occur, then we must have sufficient quantity time. Through quantity time we get those deep moments, those magic moments, those memory moments.

Bonus 2: Creating the relationships you seek

Perhaps you're thinking that it's OK when you have got a relationship to work on, but what about if you haven't even got the relationship yet? Here are ten ideas for finding the relationship you are looking for.

Idea 1: Spend one hour deciding what you want in your partner for life. And, in doing so, you will undoubtedly spend some time describing how they should look (tall, short).

All well and good. But also spend some time describing how they should be (quiet, noisy, someone who likes a discussion, a partygoer, a traveller, a foodie). What do the people you seek to meet do? For example for your set of values, beliefs and interests, would they be likely to be part of a reading group or do voluntary work, be party types or a bit of both or be theatregoers?

Idea 2: Once you know, think about where those people would spend time and join some relevant activities. The people you want to meet, what do they do, where do they go to?

Idea 3: Register online. Yes, I know you think it's mechanical; yes, I know you think it's artificial, but that doesn't mean it's not romantic. Once you know broadly who you are looking for, take every opportunity you can to increase the chances of meeting that person. Spend time researching the now vast array of online dating opportunities and preparing your profile.

Idea 4: Network. Ensure you do get out enough. I know it's harder if you are a bit of an MBTI introvert, but build your network of contacts. Go to the parties, accept the dinner invitations. The goal here is to increase your opportunities of meeting someone with whom you would like to spend more time. And remember that along the way you will probabably also create some great friendships.

Idea 5: Stay open to possibilities, especially if you have been a bit disappointed that none of those ideas seem very romantic. It is true that you can meet someone in the supermarket queue, but only if you are open-minded about the possibility. Of course, protect yourself, don't take risks. But rediscover how to be friendly. Who knows where a conversation in a busy coffee shop might lead?

Idea 6: Look after yourself. For two very good reasons. Firstly, you will be very much more attractive when you are well: you'll feel loving, romantic, sexy. And you'll look romantic, loving and sexy! Secondly, we all choose more balanced relationships when we are well: we will not be, or feel, desperate. If you have ever wondered why that friend of yours seems to keep ending up with poisonous and destructive relationships, maybe it's because they are not that 'well' most of the time.

Idea 7: Once the relationship starts, enjoy the sex, the body chemistry. It's where the initial focus tends to be, of course. It's fantastic, but also do a bit of talking. What makes your partner tick? Is this someone who could work with you in the long term or is it just some short-term fun? Don't allow the short-term, very powerful chemical buzz to cloud the longer-term wish you have.

Idea 8: In any relationship that doesn't work, ask yourself what was wrong. Was it them, or was it, in fact, you? When relationships don't work, consider whether there is a recurring pattern: is there something you do or something you seek which messes the relationship up? Can you change it or is it simply part of you and that therefore you need to adjust the relationship? Think about possible feedback.

Idea 9: Still stuck? Take a break. You're now trying too hard. There are lots of people out there. Deliberately don't look for someone and – guess what – you will find exactly the right person immediately.

Idea 10: Again – stay open-minded.

Bonus 3: How to build great relationships with your children

Be there for your children. That does not mean you are at their beck and call. Quite the reverse at times: being there for them might simply mean saying enough is enough occasionally. Make sure that they know that they are important in your life. Don't say later, don't imply they are not important. If you really can't give them the time there and then, then tell them when you can.

Be interested and interesting. Be interested in what they do. Learn key terms and words which are important to them: in their sports, their hobbies. Be interesting. Tell them about your time and what you have been up to. And if you haven't got anything interesting to say, then maybe that is some gentle feedback for you to get out more!

Arrange some formal one-to-one time with each of your children. Talk about their concerns, talk about what interests them. Discuss your work; be positive, but you don't need to be a superhero. Introduce then to some of the concerns that you have. Start the adult-to-adult relationship from the very beginning, particularly in the way that you talk to them: that is, assertively and respecting their rights. In addition:

- *Always offer unconditional love.*
- *Be loyal to your children and let them see that you are loyal to your partner.*
- *Model excellent beliefs, values and behaviours.*
- *Encourage them to seek a career/work which they will love and be passionate about.*
- *Support them with the practical aspects: ensure they have a great study/work area.*
- *Encourage music and crafts. Try and keep things like computer games in proportion.*
- *Encourage in them a love of learning, especially reading and debate.*

Bonus 4: How to be assertive

Being assertive is the perfect way to ensure your relationships go well: whether it is at work, with your teenage daughter or your spouse. To understand assertiveness we need to realize three essential concepts:

Concept 1. To be assertive is to respect rights on both sides of a conversation.

Concept 2. A right is something which is possessed either because it is a fundamental human right (such as being treated with respect) or because it is a particular right associated with the situation (perhaps a mother having the final say on what time her ten-year-old son goes to bed because she is responsible for his health).

Concept 3. There are three reasons for being assertive. It is much, much more pleasant to deal with someone in an assertive way; when we are assertive we never damage the relationship and when we are assertive we achieve the best solution that we are able to

– therefore it is likely to be implemented and likely to last. To be assertive begin to think about your rights. Here are some general rights to restore at work:

- *To express an opinion.*
- *To leave work on time.*
- *To be kept informed about the company's long-term plans.*
- *To leadership.*

And at home:

- *To have some quiet time.*
- *To have an area which is private to us.*

Now consider any specific rights you might have, such as the right to receive up-to-date data from the marketing team so that you can deliver your report on time. Implement assertive behaviour as follows:

- *Settle your own state before any interaction.*
- *Use names and give your full attention to the conversation.*
- *By all means express emotion, but don't get emotional. For example, explain how strongly you feel, but that does not give you the right to shout.*

Summary

Relationships bring us everything from joy to sadness to angst – sometimes the same relationship on the same day can bring all of those! Give your relationships attention and they will be the better for it: more joy, less haste; more up times, fewer difficult times. As organic, messy human beings we cannot predict the consistency of our relationships, nor should we try and control them. We should simply do our best to care for them.

'And, in the end, the love you take is equal to the love you make.'
Lennon and McCartney

Chapter 7
Compass Point 5: Fun

Are you having fun? Are you enjoying life? Are you happy?

When asked what we want, that's what we tend to respond: we want to be happy. Of course the definition of 'happy' varies depending on the individual you are speaking to. For some, happy is contentment, for some it is excitement, for some it is intellectual stimulation.

So, are you happy? If not, consider what isn't working, because perhaps you can change it. What's the point if you're not having fun or not having much fun? Consider that to be the bottom line, in both your personal and your business life. Put like that it's a bit of a shock for many. After all, isn't it a little impractical to be having fun with all the responsibilities they have? Jobs, careers, mortgages, families ... Others, if they are honest, don't feel that they deserve to have fun and just feel guilty when they do. And for some people there is an awful thought: 'I don't know how to have fun any more ...'

In many ways, fun is at the heart of the compass: it is the definitive motivator, the ultimate reward. But let us be clear: this fun thing will be very different for every one of us. What's fun for you? How about:

- *Going clubbing.*

- *Reading without interruptions.*
- *Hiking.*
- *Watching some old films.*
- *Spiritual connection through meditation or church.*
- *Painting.*
- *DIY.*
- *Playing with the grandchildren.*
- *Having friends round and cooking a great meal.*
- *Helping someone out who is less fortunate than you are.*
- *Building your business.*
- *Learning calculus.*

Fun is a simple and vital compass point, but it is certainly one which has been neglected by many. Simply ask yourself: 'Am I having enough fun?' If the answer is yes, then well done (we'll come back to you). If it isn't, then you'll be like many of us. Yet, as I have said, what's it all about if we're not having enough fun?

Many of us, as our responsibilities increase, begin to develop limiting beliefs: 'I simply don't have time for fun. I've got a mortgage, I'm X years old with two children'. Fine. But when will you have time for fun? Ah – quite. For others their limiting belief is that they will have fun 'one day', when they have the time, or that in business there simply isn't the time, place or inclination to have fun.

Some of you may be feeling a little smug. Maybe you're thinking that this is certainly not a compass point you need to worry about as you're having too much fun already. Three things here: firstly, don't ever lose your focus on fun, you'll be healthy and wealthy and wise. Secondly, is your fun overdose stopping you from achieving what you want to achieve? Is it at the cost of one of the other compass points, do you need to get a little more balance? You needn't lose your fun, it's probably a case of realizing that you can get fun from other elements of the compass. Thirdly, how can you use your undoubted talents to help others have more fun? Can you become a fun coach?

Is it obvious why fun is important? Perhaps. Let's just check. Fun is what makes us human; that lovely light-heartedness we can all have at times. We are enjoying life, we are focused, we have energy: our responsibilities are there but they are in balance. When we are having fun, we tend to be more creative, we tend to be able to put our concerns in balance. Fun, as we have seen, comes in many different formats: for some it is spending time with people, for others it is travelling, for others it is the business of learning. Do you know what your 'fun' is? Find it; it may be the missing piece of the jigsaw for you. It's difficult to be you, to be the authentic you, without being able to have fun.

As with so much of what we have been discussing, true fun is often internal. Of course, an exciting theme park, an evening out with friends at the theatre can be great fun and we would want this to remain so. But the ultimate fun comes when we are at one with ourselves, that is when we are feeling authentic, when we are spending time as we would wish and when we are releasing our talents, finding the artist within us.

Having more fun

How can we have more fun in our personal lives? Here are a few ideas to help you.

Allow yourself to do so. Yes, now you are big and grown up. But what do you really enjoy? What makes you laugh? Good company? A great film? Trainspotting? What? Don't give it up; bring it back. Stop feeling guilty. Ensure that you make one diary appointment every month for something that is your absolute fun. Backpacking? Watercolours? Chatting? Cooking? And think well beyond something like a drinking binge: try some healthy fun, too. Try some less predictable fun.

Develop a sense of light-heartedness. To do this make sure you get plenty of rest and relaxation. Stress stops light-heartedness. Stress develops irritability. Bonus 2 in this compass point – on flipsiding – may be particularly useful for you. Of course, always ensure that you are looking after the mind/body compass point.

Back to relationships. As we have said and seen, relationships can cause enormous fun and enormous pain in our lives. Give attention to being loving in your relationship.

Remember to bear the following statement in mind when things are proving challenging in a relationship: is it better to be loving or is it better to be right? 'Rightness' and insistence on it is a great way to destroy an important relationship because your 'right' is unlikely to be the same as your partner's. Plus, as your partner is learning and growing (see Bonus 1 later, which illustrates how important personal growth is to true fun), he or she is likely to make mistakes. Are these fundamental ones of philosophy and/or policy on which you are unable to agree or are they just differences? Rather than arguing about whether the house has been cleaned or not – you both probably have different perceptions of what is clean – agree once and for all on what makes it clean and how you will tackle it in the future. If you are differing on how the children should be educated, then set aside some time to talk about it, and continue to talk about it.

Notice how as you allow fun into your life, more fun appears. Small things can become fun. Is this all too analytical? Only if you allow it to become so.

What are the benefits of fun in your personal life?

- *You will feel better.*
- *You will be healthier.*
- *You will suffer less stress.*
- *You will have more ideas for solving problems.*
- *You will be more attractive and better company.*
- *Your relationships will improve.*
- *You will have a passion for life.*

Now, how can we have more fun in our business lives? You can allow yourself to do so and allow your team to do so. In personal interactions, try and add a little light-heartedness – you could have a fun slot or 'funny incidents' in team meetings, for example; you can encourage fun to be seen as a corporate tool for thinking differently and you can always notice the benefits of fun in creativity, innovation and conflict resolution.

What are the benefits of fun in your business life?

- *The day will be easier.*
- *Tricky relationships will be oiled.*
- *People will enjoy working with you.*
- *You are more likely to access flow states.*
- *You'll trigger some of your best and most creative states.*

Insights

Bear these in mind. One more time: the number one point is to 'allow' yourself to have fun. Yes, there is a time to work hard if we want to change our lives. And yes, it's important to consider others. But we can find that both of these issues can be addressed and still allow us time for fun. And ultimately, getting the changes you want will be fun, not work. Additionally, having fun will energize you. Having fun will build your immune system and protect you.

Be creative about how you have fun. Don't immediately think 'pub' or your favourite pastime. Notice how the most amazing fun can come from helping and supporting others – see Compass Point 6 (contribution) and Compass Point 1 (career). From a team development point of view, for example, how about putting on a charity event to support a children's home or something similar? You'll notice how motivated everyone becomes.

Finally, fun is not a waste of time. Fun is being human. To not allow fun is to not allow life.

Actions

Write down ten ways that you could start having more fun. Give this five minutes, then consider the following for some more ideas. Things you used to enjoy but have forgotten, have got rusty, feel too old and serious for:

- *Dancing.*
- *Collecting.*
- *Playing the guitar.*
- *Chatting.*

- *Gardening.*
- *Going to the cinema or theatre.*
- *DIY.*
- *Knitting.*
- *Repairing classic cars.*
- *Going to concerts.*
- *Conversation.*
- *Exploring new cities.*
- *Meeting new people.*
- *Reading great novels.*
- *Doing a course.*

Try new activities:

- *Unicycling.*
- *Juggling.*
- *Painting watercolours.*
- *Going to a museum.*
- *Reading a different author.*
- *Reconnecting with some old friends.*

Look at what you currently do, but think about doing it in different ways – for example, playing with the children actively and deciding that it's something you will enjoy.

Allow the other compass points to be fun. At work, are team meetings usually very boring? How can you change that? What can you do differently? Get some funny tapes or CDs. Keep them in the car and listen to them prior to tough sessions to warm you up.

Ask how you can have fun without money. This is especially important when spending time with children: don't allow them to feel that you need loads of money to have fun.

Keep a note of your favourite gags in the front of your notebook and always remember that fun is literally vital. Never consider it too trivial to have fun. And be surprised that fun can come from amazing sources.

How will *you* get serious about fun?

Mini case study

For Fran, the question 'are you having enough fun?' was a shock. Of course she wasn't, was anyone? But she would certainly like more. She yearned for a loving relationship. She yearned for more time to do her painting. She realized that for several years she had simply been surviving in the company in which she was working, and she needed to make a decision about that. She intended to consciously give attention to finding the relationship she sought and to getting time for her painting. Without those, she had to agree, what was the point?

Mini case study

Tim felt at a loss when the same question was put to him: he was experiencing the same dilemma now on the graduate programme as he had when he had been at university and thought everyone was having a wild time; he seemed so different from everyone else. He simply didn't like clubbing, and preferred his own company a lot of the time. An important insight for Tim was the fact that the definition of fun could be *his* definition. And, naturally, it wouldn't be the same as everyone else's definition.

Bonus section

Bonus 1: Personal development; the definitive path to fun

Remember our fundamental definition of fun? Fun is about when we are being at one with ourselves, when we are feeling authentic; when we are spending time as we would wish and when we are releasing our talents for the help and good of others, finding the artist within us. Let's take each in turn.

Being at one with ourselves means that we are happy with ourselves, we have self-confidence. We accept our lot even though we are probably attempting to improve and/or adjust it. We are increasingly internally referenced rather than externally referenced. By that I mean that we stick to our principles and are not constantly swayed by others. Spending time as we wish is critical. There is a way in which you and only you wish to spend your life. You will be happiest, you will be having the most fun when you fall into that role. Building upon that latter point, you will be at your most happiest, your most creative, you will be having the most fun when you are releasing your talents for the fun of others.

Bonus 2: 'Flipsiding', a strategy for staying light-hearted

Fun is not just about doing something. It is also about appreciating what we have, of course. It is easy to begin to notice what is not working or to be cynical or negative: to close down our minds to what is available. Flipsiding is a simple methodology which recognizes the nature of the stress reaction which can lie within all of us and which causes us to look solely at the worst aspects of a situation. Flipsiding helps us circumnavigate this when it is not helpful; let's examine it.

Stage 1: Something happens which we perceive as a threat. This might be temporarily lost car keys, an unfriendly letter from the bank manager or an angry customer. Whatever, this threatens us.

Stage 2: Evolution has developed a clever mechanism called 'fight or flight'. Fight or flight releases adrenalin and other powerful chemicals which prepare us for the approaching challenge and, in an emergency such as the need to focus on how to get out of a smoke-filled room or in a tense sporting situation such as the requirement to play really well to get to the next step of a squash ladder, they are literally invaluable. But unfortunately society has raced ahead of our genetic design. We are no longer perfectly equipped at a wired-in level for such threats in confined situations such as the car, the home or the office. And therein lies the danger: the powerful chemicals are released but we do not get a chance to 'use' them; consequently we have a physiological imbalance.

Then we get the side effects of stress, ranging from simple headaches through to poor concentration and, ultimately, possibly deeper problems.

Stage 3: What's the way out of the dilemma? Well, one route is of course to take drugs! How about paracetamol for a headache? And so on. But that, of course, is only tackling the symptom. A deeper and perhaps more elegant approach is simply to change our perception. If we don't see the event as a threat, then fight or flight will not kick in: there simply is no longer a threat.

Let's take an example: you are stuck in an appalling traffic jam, just sitting there. And the traffic news has told you that you will be there for at least two hours. What do you do? How do you look at it? Well, the first point is, of course, to accept that getting angry, irritable, whatever will not change the situation. Nor will it make you feel any better, now or when you get home. So perhaps you can flipside the situation and look at it in another way?

Let's look at this as an example. You know that you will just be sitting there, so perhaps:

- *Find a radio station you'd like to listen to – there will be one somewhere.*
- *Think about how your career is going, or try and remember who has a birthday coming up and think about a present.*
- *Assuming it's legal to do so, phone someone who doesn't get to hear from you as much as either of you would like.*
- *Assuming it's safe, get out and have a stretch; chat to neighbouring drivers.*
- *Tidy the car.*
- *Look at the road atlas – so that's where Inverness/York/Padstow is ...*

Of course, if it's a stop–start traffic jam, you will have fewer options – but you do still have some.

Now try these two situations. Compare your thoughts with some suggested ones over the page:

Situation 1: Angry customer

For some reason you have got a very angry customer on the phone. It is nothing to do with you personally, but the fact is that you have got this person shouting at you. Now, clearly you don't want to be talking to this individual, but given that you are, what are you going to do, in particular to flipside it?

Situation 2: Romantic weekend

The plan had been for a romantic weekend. Unfortunately, early on Saturday morning when the post arrives, there's a letter from the bank manager about the unauthorized overdraft on your joint account. Your initial feelings are of irritation with your partner. How can you act but at the same time not spoil the weekend?

Thoughts on situation 1: Angry customer

It's only feedback. Thank goodness that we have heard from this person: maybe we can now address the issue. It's a chance to use our skills; we've been on the course, read the book, seen the video. Now's here's an opportunity to do it for real. Research suggests that advocates – individuals who express huge admiration for a company and a service – are often ones who have experienced poor service in the first place. You can turn this round. Imagine how good you will feel and how well set up for the job you will feel when you handle this well. Imagine how your reputation will spread .

Thoughts on situation 2: Romantic weekend

Once again it is, after all, feedback. There's clearly something wrong: the bank has got it wrong or cash flow is wrong. But there's probably no need to deal with it absolutely at this moment. Enjoy the weekend. But towards the end, when you are both feeling very mellow, could be a great time to discuss it. Hopefully any defensiveness will have dissolved: whatever, now would be a really good time to begin to resolve this issue. It's a test of how good your relationship is. Do you go into blame mode or can you stay loving and work something through?

Bonus 3: Understanding the times you are not having fun

Please, please don't think that you must always be cheerful, that you must always be happy, that you must always be positive. That is not human either. There are a whole range of human emotions including ones such as sadness, depression, anger, guilt and fear. Every single one of them exists for a good reason. We should not try and pretend that they are not there, we should not try and camouflage them. Instead use them to return to our natural state.

Perhaps a simple analogy will help. Have you ever had flu? What are the symptoms you remember, maybe aching and high temperature? Those symptoms are a real nuisance, but again they are there for a reason. The aches and pains sensitize you so that you go to bed and lie down. The high temperature helps to kill the virus. And if you do go to bed and rest and drink plenty of water, you will get better. You can always camouflage those symptoms with a flu remedy and then you'll wonder why you are still not feeling that great in a few week's time. Let's look at some emotions in the same way. For example:

- *Sadness. This is there to cause us to reflect, to take stock, to help us think back on happy times. Use it to allow and direct that reflective nature.*
- *Fear. This is a check: is this safe? Do I want to move on? But equally fear can be a spur: what am I going to do, then?*
- *Anger. This can be a motivator: I want to do something. Then do so; use the tremendous energy anger can generate to get the change you want or work to right the wrong.*
- *Depression. This is feedback, assuming it's not chronic depression. Something is up, something is not right. It's a trigger, provoking you into sorting something out.*

Summary

To have fun – in your own way – is to be human. There will, of course, be times in your life when there perhaps seems to be a lack of fun, but don't allow that to be the norm. Have fun!

Chapter 8

Compass Point 6: Contribution

The first five compass points are concerned with our immediate perspective: our personal world of work, our family and friends, our wellness, our most immediate concerns. Compass Point 6: Contribution, takes a different viewpoint: it is concerned with looking beyond our immediate remit and considering the bigger picture – be that a team of which we are a part, our family or even the world at large, with a wider (what are the implications of my actions?) and deeper (what's really going on here?) perspective. It's the compass point which encourages us to acknowledge that we are always part of something larger – a system – and that our thoughts and actions will always impact – eventually – all the parts of that system. We are all part of many such systems, for example:

- *A family.*
- *A team.*
- *A band.*
- *An organization.*
- *A community.*
- *A virtual team.*
- *The environment.*

Those are the macrosystems of which we are a part. Daily, of course, we work and interact in microsystems such as:

- *A meeting.*
- *A conversation.*
- *An argument.*

Some of these are regular and permanent, others are infrequent and temporary.

In essence, this compass point asks how you are supporting the systems of which you are a part. Or, even more simply, how are you contributing? Are you a systems thinker or not?

Understanding Compass Point 6 and its implications is a significant breakthrough for many individuals as they struggle to understand why, despite their hard work, some of their dreams are not yet being realized. Or maybe why a simple action which was beneficial to them, a colleague or a member of their family seemed to upset and/or annoy so many others, or why an apparently sensible quick-fix decision has dire consequences down the line. This is perhaps because, quite simply, they are not yet noticing the full implications of their actions.

Mini case study

Pat loves the work she does: she's a designer at a top design agency. But she regularly states how she hates both the way clients are treated behind the scenes and the pressure she is put under when she is meant to be coming up with something creative. Both of those may be very valid points, but unfortunately Pat has a tendency to sulk in team meetings and put across her views in an non-constructive way. She gets labelled as negative and 'not a contributor'. Pat is not seeing the system of which she is a part. She is not seeing that the way she is has as much of an impact as what she says.

Mini case study

Rex loves the pretty Berkshire village in which he lives, but he does get frustrated that some of his neighbours don't pull their weight when handling issues. For example, he has blamed a lot of his neighbours for allowing their children to play and picnic down by the newly established village pond and leave litter there. Rex undoubtedly has a point, but blaming these people behind their back and judging them responsible just because they have children is unlikely to help. Currently Rex is not a 'contributor' thinker.

Insights

Compass Point 6 encourages us to see the impact of our actions, particularly beyond their immediate consequences. This is, of course, a particularly powerful emotional intelligence or 'EQ' skill: the ability to look at the longer-term consequences of our actions and if necessary to defer gratification. Deferring gratification sounds as if it means taking the fun away, being serious, but it doesn't mean that at all. It simply means being willing to defer the quick fix you get now for much, much bigger benefits in the long term. When we drop a piece of chewing gum on the ground, what are the implications of that action? Immediately, perhaps, no big deal. And we do get the pleasure of getting rid of the annoyance of having to hold that sticky bit of paper and might even have a slight feeling of having got away with something which we are not really supposed to do. The implications are small: irritation to someone as the gum gets caught on their shoe. But then the implications begin to multiply: we get frustrated with our pavements looking less attractive and our city's cleaning bills increasing. One simple action: dropping the gum. The consequences: potentially vast. Here's another example. Surely it's no big thing if I chose not to invest in a pension fund at the moment? After all I'm only 29; plenty of time for that boring stuff later. Immediately, perhaps, it is no big deal. But no saver habit is being established, no planning habit is being reinforced, no financial discipline is being built. And perhaps, most easily, the money is not being saved when its multiplier effect will be huge. Compass Point 6 encourages us to regularly review and ensure that we are supporting each and every system of which we are a part, and that in particular we consider the short-, medium- and long-term implications of our actions.

This contribution compass point encourages us to be more of a connections thinker. Here's another example. As a family we seem to be in a lot of tension, what are the causes of that? We're clearly not communicating that well, and that's because we don't see each other, and that's because we no longer have meals together, and that's because people want to watch different TV programmes at different times, and that's because … Maybe we should have some times when television is banned and get everyone more proficient at recording the programmes they want to watch later. Is it time to stop and sort some of this mess out? What can we do?

The contribution compass point supports our effectiveness through anticipation. Thus: 'I don't think the team is going to like this announcement. How can I help them? What are going to be their key concerns? Naturally many of them will probably feel this is a sneaky way to prepare the ground for redundancies. I want to convince them, that although change is certainly necessary, redundancy is not the thing we have in mind.'

Let's take a look in more detail at some of the systems which I mentioned, and with each, take some reflection points, looking in particular at the connections to which we may wish to give more attention.

In a family

What could each of us, but particularly 'I' do to make things easier in the family? What might I be doing instead of blaming? Do we get any quality time together as a family? Do we talk about the frustrations of living together? Do I get any quality time with my partner?

What are your individual mission statements, that is what are you personally trying to achieve over and above day-to-day survival and paying the mortgage? What is your joint mission statement – where do you want to take your lives? What are some of the exciting things you wish to do? How can you help your children in a tough and demanding world? Do you spend decent one-to-one time with each of your children? Remember the wretched quality time–quantity time debate and be careful. For work, go for quality time: be there as little as you can and do an outstanding job. For home, strive for quantity time so you can allow those magic moments to happen, those important conversations to flow. Have you asked each of your children things like how you could make their life better and/or easier? What values and beliefs are you instilling in your children? Here are some stories to clarify this point.

Story 1: Your daughter arrives home from school in a very excited mood having attended a talk at school from an enthusiastic Police Constable. She is enthused and committed; what more could you ask as parents – she's a new, committed citizen? The next day, driving to visit her grandparents, your speed hits 90. Your daughter yells out: 'You're breaking the speed limit!'. Ahh – a moment of truth! How do you respond? Laugh? Say 'but everyone does it'? Or are you willing to apologize, slow down and both respect the law, your daughter's observations and the integrity of your values?

Story 2: Your child overhears you talking to your partner and saying 'Well, I'll try and put it through on expenses. Strictly speaking, we weren't allowed to stay both nights at the Christmas do, but they'll be so busy processing all the stuff that I expect it'll get through'. What's the message to your child? If you can get away with it, do it?

Story 3: You are fed up because one of your children's teachers seems to be ignoring a lot of the potential in your child, but as you converse with the teacher you start shouting: you are displaying similar behaviours to the ones you are complaining about.

Think connections: where is this leading me?

Are you focusing, in the family, on quantity time out of which will pop those magic moments? And what about all the great family times: do you recall them? Do you remind everyone to think about what is going well for them? What are the rituals that are so important? Things like the ridiculous, badly decorated Christmas cake; the walk in the dark on bonfire night. Whatever they are, conserve the rituals and enjoy them as magical times. Don't allow Disney or whatever to dictate yours. That's not to say that Disney can't be a great deal of fun, but don't let it determine your family culture and family rituals.

In a team

How can I support others and live and breathe the mission? Do I show up for what is necessary? Do I maintain loyalty to everyone, especially those who are not present? Do we have a 'plastic' vision statement, that is one which is simply a plaque on the wall and which everyone ignores, or does everyone in the team live and breathe it? Do we have clear PPL: purpose, process and leadership? Do we see the connections between what we talk about and what we focus on and what we achieve?

Think about leadership, and notice that the term is very much leadership not just 'a leader'. Leadership is concerned with each individual in the team taking absolute personal responsibility for what they are doing: for seeing the connections of how they behave with the results that they will get. Think about how you lead and manage. Is it by being focused on what is important, by shouting, by reacting? Or are you one of the team, constantly talking about what is not being done but on the other hand not doing anything yourself?

In an organization

Ask yourself: am I a cynic, regularly destroying through my words the efforts of others? Or am I a contributor, working to help others? If I don't like things, what am I doing to change them? Or why don't I go and start afresh? Do I raise my good ideas and push them through? Am I seen as an innovator? When I go on a course do I use the skills I learn or do I stick the folder on the shelf and stagnate? Am I an enthuser?

In a community

Are you a complainer or a contributor? Could you attend some of the community meetings? Maybe they would be less of a 'they' if you knew who they were. Are you the aloof one? Do you say 'hello' to your neighbours? No? And do you then sigh deeply as you watch the evening news and notice the decay of our communities?

In a relationship

Ask what your partner needs from you in order to make it an even better relationship. Have you sat down and shared these compass ideas? Or have you just assumed that they would be against what you are trying to do? Are you open to their exciting ideas of changing jobs, writing a book – or have you judged them to be 'ridiculous'? What is your definition of love? Are you willing to explore the idea that true love might be supporting them in realizing their vision?

In the environment

Do you despair when you hear what has happened at the latest Earth Conference (usually nothing)? Or do you decide to do something yourself such as recycle paper, recycle bottles? And, yes, maybe you have heard that it actually makes no difference at all and that we would be better off simply putting them into landfills. Recycle your woollen goods, then, because even that will make a difference. And have you stopped using plastic bags at the supermarket and use cardboard boxes or recycle bags instead?

And do you choose your suppliers carefully? Whose jam, whose sweets do you buy? Of course it's not easy. Of course some cynical marketers exploit our desires for such services and products, but don't let that put you off. Research as best you can and make the best decisions you can. How about in the work environment? Could you recycle more? What about paper, ink cartridges?

And what about being a contributor on a broader scale? Perhaps:

- *Set up a standing order for your favourite charity.*
- *Increase the amount of your charity's standing order if you've already established one.*
- *Buy* The Big Issue *every week.*
- *Give some time to a voluntary organization.*
- *Have a contribution mindset:*

  - *Become less judging.*
  - *Become more accepting.*
  - *Think about and respect the environment.*
- *Try some random (and anonymous) acts of kindness:*
  - *Let an older person with not much in their basket go in front of you in the supermarket queue.*

Mini case study

Agusto had so much: the flat, the car, but he yearned for something more. The contribution point rang so true, currently more so than any of the others. It was the missing point in his compass. But, what? What could he contribute? He grabbed his black notebook and his fat black fountain pen and scribbled in his fast, forward-facing script:

- *be nice to others.*
- *be courteous to others.*
- *learn the key phrases in the language of the countries which I visit: 'please', 'thank you', 'that was a very good meal', 'goodbye' – and use them.*
- *be accepting and less judging.*
- *ring my sister and chat to her.*

He did those and he felt great. He continued to add to his list every day. He felt more real, more authentic.

Mini case study

James ran a small consultancy. High fees, long hours. His employees often seemed close to burning out. He had tried holding a few workshops around work/life balance and productivity for the team. The last one he ran was my Personal Excellence; it rang true and he decided to get a small community project off the ground. The results were amazing. Doing some basic work in the local old people's home restored a sense of humility. It reduced some of the egos. It was transforming.

What are the benefits of being a contributor or systems thinker?

It often initially appears that this compass point is about being a bit of a 'goody two-shoes'. Does it really have a place in the tough world of business and what are the benefits for the practitioner? The answer is certainly that it does: the world of work needs this kind of thinking more than ever. It can be seen in:

- *Possibility thinking: thinking connections and building those connections networks – where does this take us? What might happen here?*
- *Alliance thinking: who can we work with?*
- *Abundance thinking: rather than simply trying to get a bigger slice of pie, actually making the pie bigger.*
- *Network and/or niche thinking.*

And the benefits for you as an individual are clear:

- *Personal development, particularly in the areas of personal effectiveness and possibility thinking.*
- *Emotional intelligence, particularly in level one of emotional intelligence, which is self-awareness.*
- *Building your own personal network of connections.*

Actions

What actions will *you* take?

Bonus section

Bonus 1: Ten ways to develop a fantastic family culture

1 Offer unconditional love to each member of your family. Love them for who they are; resist the temptation to judge them simply because they think in a different way, have differing dreams and differing experience. That does not mean, of course, that

you accept inappropriate behaviour. Ensure your children have clear guidelines. Talk to your partner and share your values, dreams and vision, and agree the best ways to develop and coach your children. Be accepting of each other's views.

2 Allow plenty of 'talk time'. Talk about the news, food, holidays and special days, what everyone is reading, what is happening at school, college and work. Mealtimes are an excellent oportunity for such discussions; ensure that from an early age children know that it is not acceptable to slink off to their room with a tray of food. Consider carefully the balance between interaction time and computer/TV time.

3 Set aside a formal family meeting time to discuss good news and difficult matters. 'Rotate' the chair from the earliest age. Have an agenda such as this: everyone's news, problems anyone wants to mention, diary sharing (who is doing what, when and who would like who to come to their play/football match). Keep a record and ensure promised actions are carried out.

4 Allow and recognize difference in the family. The chatty one, the loving one, the detached one, the noisy one, the downright difficult one. As a parent work to support each of them.

5 Talk adult-to-adult all the time, even to the youngest toddler. Treat them with respect, be willing to apologize for your (many) mistakes and help them build their own lives.

6 Develop early responsibilities: ask everyone to help with family tasks. Ensure everyone knows how to use the washing machine, do the washing up or how to operate the dishwasher. Encourage the use of public transport and getting around on their own. Not only does it encourage responsibility, it'll keep them fit, resourceful and develop their planning skills.

7 Develop and encourage family rituals, whatever they are, from sharing meals to celebrating birthdays and going to church at Christmas.

8 Encourage 'one-to-ones' or times when family members get together for some time with just one other person.

9 Keep a wall planner with everyone's coming and goings marked on it; ensure it is up to date and insist on certain times when you are all together.

10 Respect your own down time and privacy with your partner. You may have become mum and dad, but you are still young and in love – or at least you are if you give yourself a chance.

Bonus 2: Ten ways to develop a high-performing team

1 Check that the team has a mission, knows what its purpose is, what its point is and what it is trying to do.

2 Check that everyone knows what the mission is and is able to live and breathe it, and that they feel they know how to put it into action.

3 Ensure that you get involved in one-to-one discussions with everyone on the team. Use these as times to coach and overcome any challenges to people doing their best work.

4 Develop the mantra of 'plan-do-review'. In particular, review after every session and decide what can be learnt. Be not just a high-performance team, but a high-performance learning team.

5 Ensure every member of the team has a clear personal development plan, especially one which is focused clearly on career.

6 Write a team charter, essentially a code of conduct, and decide clearly what is expected of each person in the team.

7 Invest in the team: encourage them to read valuable personal development materials and send them on training sessions.

8 At team meetings, regularly ask these questions: 'On a scale of one to five, where one is simply a collection of individuals and five is a high-performance team, where do you feel we are? Assuming we are not yet a five, what needs to be done to close the gap?'

9 Encourage team members to spend time with other teams finding out how they work.

10 Encourage team members to develop their own niches, their own growth paths. Be honest with them in giving praise. Be honest with them in where they need to improve.

Bonus 3: How to become a systems thinker in five easy steps

1 Consider the implications of your actions. Any action or step you take will reverberate around the office and home. Sometimes in a loud, dramatic way; sometimes in a quiet, discreet way. But it will do so. Before you take any action, ask who and what will this impact on in the longer term, and whether that is all right.
2 Remember that the implications are not always as simple as you might wish, whether it's your relationship with your teenage son or global politics. Thus in an attempt to encourage more discipline in your daughter's study habits, you ground her. Consequently, she does no studying. Begin to notice that sometimes, whatever you intend, the reverse happens.
3 Be willing to defer your gratification in the short term for the longer term.
4 Be clear on your personal vision.
5 Keep a notebook and use it to reflect on what kind of month it has been at the end of every one. Month by month you will notice how you become a more effective systems thinker.

Bonus 4: The personal LifeCompass as a system

It will probably have not escaped your notice that the compass itself is of course a system: any attention to one part has significant implications elsewhere. We'll get to that a little later, after we have looked at the LifeCompass in daily use.

Summary

Contribute. Become a systems thinker; consider the consequences of your steps. It will make both your life and the lives of others easier.

Chapter 9
LifeCompass: Every Day

Before we move to the big picture, the one of full integration and synergy between each of the compass points, let's fast forward to how we can actually use the compass on a daily basis.

The LifeCompass is our guide; it helps us get out of life what we want to get out of it. It does not control us: it frees us. Always remember, as I pointed out earlier, that if you do not set your personal compass, then someone else will have set it for you; it may be, for example, that your personal compass is effectively your inbox! Let's review it at the most strategic level and then get more tactical.

Stage 1: Monthly review

Do a major review of your LifeCompass once a month. Each month ask those questions through which I have guided you, the power questions. As a result of your responses, detail your goals for each compass point and the actions necessary. Consider both the long term (for example, 'start my own business') and the short term ('achieve quality targets this month'). Notice sticking points, for instance a promotion still not achieved. Decide to give extra attention to those points. Ask a specific question: 'What is blocking me here and consequently, what do I need to do?' The monthly review is simply a guide. When and if you are undergoing a lot of change in your life you may want to review your compass weekly or even more frequently. And I would certainly expect that following your study of this material you will want to consider your compass points frequently, at least initially. For ease, the main compass power questions are summarized at the end of this stage.

If you are in a close relationship, encourage your partner to answer the compass questions, too. Perhaps answer them separately, then spend a bit of time together and notice any overlap and difference. In any healthy relationship there will be differences of opinion; the point of the compass is not to try and get the same answers. The point of the compass is to give some thought to the individual lives you are living and how you might support each other in your respective dreams. Eventually you might wish to use the compass as a basis for the crucial decisions you need to make.

Should you have children, then as they get to secondary school age encourage them to begin to think about their LifeCompass, too. It will give them a useful perspective and framework for the career, exam and life battles ahead. It will encourage them to think outside the box of school subjects and exams.

Do a 'first pass capture' of the actions which you feel are necessary to take. You may want to do it now.

Compass power questions: summary

Compass Point 1: Career

- *Where do you want your career to be in three years' time? (If it's a beach bar in Australia you wish to be running, that's what gets written down.)*
- *What three specific actions can you take over the next four months to ensure that this happens?*
- *Is your CV updated? If you are not updating your CV every month, start doing so now.*
- *Take ten minutes out and answer the question 'why would anyone want to*

employ me?'. Look for five positive, strong reasons; ensure there is a mixture of hard skills (for example, how to define and run a two-million-dollar project) and soft skills (the ability to remotivate a disillusioned team leader).

- *Are you working with passion? Start looking for the intrinsic worth in everything you do: whatever you do, do it with passion or stop doing it.*

Compass Point 2: Mind/body

- *Use the context of MEDS to review progress on this compass point. For each point of MEDS, what is one action you might take?*
- *Specifically:*
  - *M – Are you taking time out and investing in yourself, every day?*
  - *E – Are you building cardiovascular exercise into your day? Not only will you feel better, you'll have a clear desire to take action.*
  - *D – Are you eating for energy and long-term health? Have you stopped eating rubbish?*
  - *S – Are you reducing, perhaps eliminating, any sleep debt?*
- *Are you practising choosing your state and looking for the flipside?*

Compass Point 3: Finance

- *What rating do you give your finances, from one to ten? Decide three specific actions you can take within the next six months to improve your rating.*
- *Specifically:*
  - *Be clear that you and your partner understand the difference between quality of life and standard of living.*
  - *Decide your personal financial independence day.*
  - *Start keeping a personal financial balance sheet.*

Compass Point 4: Relationships

- *What relationships would you like to improve? And how might you do it?*

- *Review each of your important one-to-one relationships. Distinguish them clearly from the one-to-many relationships.*
- *For each one-to-one relationship, review the Five As of great relationships: attention, awareness of difference, appreciation, affection and action.*

Compass Point 5: Fun

- *Are you having fun? If not, start now.*
- *Define fun more broadly: consider your career, consider contribution.*

Compass Point 6: Contribution

- *What systems are you a part of?*
- *Are you acting as a positive contributor to them?*

Stage 2: Balance LifeCompass

Check that appropriate balance is being given across all compass points. For example, if you have decided that you are going to have a six-month push on getting promotion, how will you ensure you do not neglect your family at the same time? Or your exercise routine? Maybe stepping back from one compass point would give you the breakthrough which you are looking for. Remember, every compass point change will have implications elsewhere. However, don't feel that you only have a certain amount of time and that therefore you can only focus on one compass point at a time. As the compass points begin to synergize you begin to make and realize time.

Stage 3: Consider major decisions against the compass

One example could be education for the children. What sort of education do you want for them? And given that, what will be the consequences elsewhere? Every major decision will have implications across the compass.

Stage 4: Create a master list mapped against the compass

In the next part I'll look at the concept of a master list in more detail. This stage is the one where you can start using it effectively. At the beginning of each week, plan the forthcoming week and set priorities on your master list. Ensure that it is increasingly driven by compass actions. Initially your master list will probably be holding a considerable number of important and urgent (that is, clock) activities. In a year's time it will be predominantly compass driven, including more important and investing activities (my earlier book *Being the Best* has more on those ideas).

Stage 5: Extend your planning horizon

Consider where you want to be in 5 years, 10 years, even 25 years. A little thought now will certainly help it happen. Again, this is in no way losing spontaneity. The goal is to give you more spontaneity. Poor planning is what often causes someone to have restricted options and not be able to make their way forward with what they truly want to do.

Chapter 10
The Master List

Regular consideration of the LifeCompass will of course generate actions. Capture these on your master list which I mentioned briefly in the last piece. This is your simple, pragmatic day-to-day tool which helps you both 'do' what is necessary and also 'be' what is important. It makes it straightforward to be a compass thinker; it allows you to make compass thinking something which you live and breathe.

Please be aware that a master list is absolutely, definitely not a 'to do' list. A to do list is short term, urgent and reactive. As we shall see, a master list is a lot more than that. There is nothing intrinsically wrong with a to do list. We eventually do need to do stuff. However that is only a sub-set on our master list.

Here are the characteristics of the master list. I'll look at potential formats in a moment.

Complete and absolute

Your master list is a list of everything: short term, long term, wishes, dreams, home and work. Everything to which you need to give attention is on that list (maybe plans for the family summer holiday). Everything to which you think you might want to give attention is on that list (such as plans for a business start-up). Do not hold anything in your head that you do not need to do. Allow your brain to do what it's best at: think intelligently and be creative. Importantly, all your hopes and plans and wishes from your compass consideration will go onto this master list. Do not be concerned that they are not urgent. That is the point. They are not urgent, they are investing. Your master list is your primary decision-making tool; you defer to nothing else, apart from the odd emergency, the odd crisis. Your master list represents your best thinking; your best committments. Your life will be guided by your best thinking and consideration which is captured on your master list. It is not driven by your inbox, your in-tray or crises caused by poor planning.

Portable

Is it with you at all times? If it's not then you will not be able to capture items on it, nor will you be able to review it. And think about what portable really means: truly so. It must be on you or with you at all times.

Home and work

One of the reasons people lose balance in their lives is that they have no focus on what they want to do outside work. Don't separate the lists into subjects, otherwise when the pressure is on, which one will you look at? That's right: work.

No organization

Do not waste time putting tasks into various sections or deciding their priorities at this stage. This is simple capture only. The organization and implementation come later.

How do you use the master list? Simply review it each end of day, ten minutes before you leave work and 'break and date'. By break and date I mean take any task which is not brain friendly (which you do not feel it is easy enough to do, which is not attractive enough to do) and is not time friendly (will not fit into a 20-minute chunk which is currently all you can find) and break it down until it is. Then schedule it by allocating a start date.

Creating momentum: setting life vision and overcoming blockers

You now have your LifeCompass beginning to take shape. You might find it helpful to take make your own version of the LifeCompass diagram in Figure 10.1. The outer perimeter is the value at which you feel you could do no more. The innermost points are those which need maximum attention.

This gives you two things. Firstly, an indicator of where to give more attention. Also, in a few months time, you can begin to notice where progress is being made. Take a look at your compass. What's the big picture for you? What's your life vision? What's your purpose? Create a statement.

How to create a personal mission statement

Ensure that you get some time to yourself. Take a pen and a piece of paper and writing as quickly as you can, note down the intentions that you have. What do you wish to achieve? Write, write, write. Now leave it for a complete day and then come back to it.

Here are some examples from recent programmes which I have run:

- *We want to start a family and we're not going to let this crazy business about needing enough money stop us.*

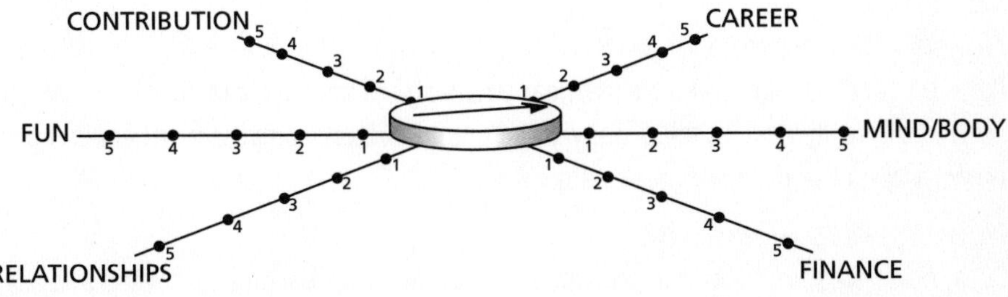

Figure 10.1 LifeCompass

- *I AM going to start my own business within six months.*
- *I will re-invent my current lifestyle so that I have: 1. more energy, 2. more fun.*
- *I want to get promotion and have my own team.*

Write and rewrite your vision. Here are some more examples:

- *My focus for the next 18 months is to get my health back but without neglecting the health of my family.*
- *I am determined to get my true job, my true dharma. I feel inspired that I am en route.*

Keep your personal mission statement visible in a study area.

Now, what might stop you?

Will anything stop you realizing your vision and getting your compass to work? Let's just spend a while on what might stop you. In my experience, these are the top five blockers that you may believe that you have to deal with.

How exactly do I start?

Simply start. You'll learn loads as you go along. The feeling of being unsure is natural. The desire to have the complete picture before starting is also natural. But, back to the beginning: pencil and paper. Laptop, keyboard. Conversation in a café with a trusted friend, that's how you get clarity. Start. Then come back to this book. Then do some more.

How do I get the energy to do it?

If this is your challenge, you have the clear advantage of knowing exactly what work you need to do: really work at mind/body. Read the mind/body compass point again. Focus on getting your body into a great state.

How do I keep motivated?

Start, don't wait until you are motivated – you may never become so! Start, and then you'll be motivated.

How do I find the time?

That's exactly what this is all about. You'll never have enough time; but you can have sufficient direction.

What might people think as I begin to change?

On this occasion, forget them. Get on with what you know is important.

Chapter 11

LifeCompass: Integration and Synergy

You now have a deeper level of understanding of the six compass points. To help understanding we have taken one compass point at a time, explored its implications and agreed some actions in that area. This has ensured clear direction. However, as I said at the start, we also need balance across the compass points. So in a moment we'll be taking an overview and seeing if there is any fine-tuning we need to do to bring the six points into balance. By balance, I mean recognizing that progress in one area of our life might – but not necessarily – mean potential degradation in another area, the simplest example being that of giving extra time to one area may mean less time for another.

Through this consideration we hope that we will not only avoid conflict between compass points but also ideally gain something more – synergy – between them. By this I mean the ability to use one compass point to help another. A simple example might be how resolving conflict in a relationship immediately helps with mind/body. Here are some other examples.

Example 1. When we focus on career and decide what is important to us and start to achieve it, we immediately feel more purposeful and energetic, hence our mind/body feels more fully alive. A fully alive mind/body enables us to get done what it is necessary to do, it creates a natural inclination for action. This, of course, is essential for the overall achievement of the compass points.

Example 2. As we give more direction and focus to mind/body, we feel more relaxed and more positive about the possibilities open to us and are happier in our relationships, even when they are at their most trying. As our relationships improve and we feel happier, once again we are more inclined to take the decisions and actions we need to take. In addition, a relationship which isn't working is very time consuming: as our relationships work we have more time to enjoy them and the other aspects of our full lives.

Example 3. When we give direction and focus to finance, we begin to realize that we can contribute a lot more to others. As we contribute to others our eyes and consequently our minds are opened; we gain a more mature perspective of the world.

Example 4. When we begin to contribute, we begin to realize a bigger picture: things fall into place, we are able to put various aspects in proportion and life becomes a whole lot easier.

Example 5. When we start to do what we want in our career, we start to have more fun. When we are having fun, the whole area becomes a whole lot more relaxed, our relationships improve and we feel more energized.

One reason we often don't get the life we would wish to have is that we only develop (and even that development has often been unconscious) one compass point, and that is so often career. Balance is respecting the push and pull of the compass points. When we consider the compass holistically, that is when we gain the energy to be successful.

Steadily, day by day, week by week and month by month, we give attention to each compass point. Naturally we get benefits from improvement on that particular compass point, but what is also exciting is how we get improvement across all the compass points. Each begins to reinforce the others.

As we give attention to each compass point, it develops, others develop. As others develop we notice synergy and it all takes off.

And now …

You're ready. Take action, read more and try and attend a workshop. But above all, start! Good luck!

(I suggest that when you are ready – probably not exactly now – come back and read the next section. It's best considered when you have been implementing the compass for a while.)

Chapter 12
LifeCompass: Evolution?

Taking LifeCompass to the next stage: welcome back!

Just a reminder: this section is not an essential part of your first read. In fact it is probably best considered when you have spent a few months working with your compass.

The initial power of the compass came through attention and focus. There is now a second level of benefit available to us which derives from the integration and holistic approach of the compass. As attention is given to one particular point, that helps with another. As one point makes progress, they all make progress. How can we make progress on mind/body if we haven't sorted out career? How can we be having fun if we aren't making progress on relationships? This is exciting and very good news. Originally, although we were committed, we thought it was going to be very hard work. But we are now finding a tremendous multiplier effect. Attention to one is attention to all.

Advanced LifeCompass principle 1

Attention to one compass point is immediately equivalent to attention to all the other compass points. This attention may be empowering or hindering; be sensitive to it. This attention will multiply the attention we are giving to the compass.

The compass points are so strongly interrelated that they always impact on each other. Here's an example. You get promoted. That's clearly a huge step on the career compass point. What might the implications be in each of the other compass points?

Mind/body: will the promotion possibly cause more stress? Probably more buzz, initially? What will the long-term workload be like? Is any training available for skill development to help with the extra demands?

Finance: will the promotion make more money available? And after taxes and extra commuting and having to buy lunch in a more expensive area, will it be worth it? Will this help? Does it overcome old debt or does it raise new expectations about what can be spent?

Relationships: will there be new people to work with, new networks to build and possibly less time at home? Possibly the commute will be shorter or it might be fine to work at home one day a week.

Fun: will there initially be less time for personal interests? Perhaps those will be less important anyway as the new area of work becomes more stimulating.

Contribution: what will this change require? Maybe being more or less of a team player; and what about some of the outside work recently developed; can that continue?

Advanced LifeCompass principle 2

Progress on one compass point sometimes leads to a temporary setback on another. The compass may need to be realigned for a fully 'congruent' compass.

Given that our compass has often had so little attention for a while, it is not surprising that the previously settled system throws up some difficulties upon disturbance. Just as an unhealthy body often initially feels worse during detox, a non-aligned, non-synergistic compass takes time to 'rebalance'. As the example above shows, a dramatic promotion might mean that stress levels go up initially and gym sessions are missed. That, of course, means that the mind/body compass point is being damaged. Consequently that compass point will need to be addressed.

Advanced LifeCompass principle 3

Compass 'magic' starts when we move from level 1 compass attention to level 2 compass attention.

By compass 'magic' I mean that we start getting very strong synergy and 'quantum leap' breakthroughs on each of the points. It was natural that initially we would consider each compass point at its most fundamental level: for ease of understanding, ease of learning and ease of implementation. Let's look at them each in turn.

Career

Ideally we are now focused on doing work which we increasingly enjoy and develops us. This is occurring via a two-pronged approach: firstly, seeking the work we love; secondly, whatever the work we are currently doing, we act and treat it as if we love it. We have put aside limiting beliefs about what we can or can't do or what qualifications we need and have decided to simply pursue our dreams. As Joseph Campbell says: 'follow your bliss'. It's true that we will undoubtedly be led by our talents, but we do not allow those to be our only deciding factor.

We do not expect perfection on the path, but we do notice that we are enjoying our work more and more. We feel valued, we feel we are contributing. Work becomes less of something which we 'do', less of a separate and disparate part of our life. It becomes something which is integrated into our life instead. And although once we used to worry about work and consequently think about it 24/7, we now just see it as something which is part of us and certainly not something to worry about. Yes, sure it comes to mind; but only as any other aspect of our life might do.

This is the beginning of finding our way to true dharma or life purpose. As I discussed earlier, this is the job/career/activity which engages us fully, about which we are passionate, which once we are actually doing it is so obvious ... Through it we consolidate our authenticity and allow our spirit – the very essence of us – to be released. If 'spirit' seems an odd term to be using in the area of career development, remind yourself how easily we use the term 'lacking spirit'. We all know that there is something deeper to this business of work: it's our spirit. Engaged or not. Growing or not. Passionate or not.

As we continue to give attention to our true career and find that work becomes easier, opportunities present themselves and we are no longer constantly struggling. We notice that career supports mind/body and is no longer separate. It helps our intellectual development and reflection. It drives our finances and encourages a new 'affluence' thinking. Our relationships at work and home are certainly better because of our new career. Fun and contribution are taken care of. We see how critically important career is in our thinking and development: but not because of money. Because of affluence. Because of abundance. Our compass point for career is becoming more fully aligned.

Now is a good time to introduce the concept of the levels of alignment. It is possible to have three degrees of alignment with each compass point:

- *Level 0 is the level at which we are not thinking compass, we are not thinking about our life either holistically or synergistically. We are simply experiencing it.*
- *Level 1 is the level at which we become engaged with our purpose and gain benefits through attention to and synergy across the compass points.*
- *Level 2 is the level at which we truly 'be', the level at which we become authentic.*

In terms of Compass Point 1: Career:

- *At level 0 we possess a job/career; it is something we do. The most significant motivation is 'the package'; we have a set of skills which we develop and which are very much seen as an add-on to who we are. Even our interpersonal skills are seen as techniques, especially of winning and manipulation.*
- *At level 1 our career becomes something which is very important to us; it is who we are. The motivation is less for the package, but more for how our career*

nurtures us and develops us. Career/dharma, be; at level 1 we have begun to recognize and release our talents.

- *At level 2 our career becomes something which releases the 'artist' in us: dharma/ 'bliss'; be here, now; spirit; entrepreneur/artist; contribution. The package we receive is merely a measure.*

I'll look at the three levels for each of the other compass points. And with each one I'll ask the question of how we can move from a lower level to a higher level – so let's first complete that piece of work for career.

How do we move from level 1 to level 2? The key here is the appearance of entrepreneurial spirit. Don't panic: this doesn't necessarily mean starting your own business. What it does mean is a new mindset. The entrepreneurial mindset is a mindset in which we are proactive, deliver excellence and take ownership. Once we think entrepreneur, then everything falls into place. As an entrepreneur we invest in ourselves – everything we can. We are innovative and creative. If you are a team leader, you get your team to think business; if you are a receptionist you think 'If I were working for myself as a contract receptionist, what would I be doing if I were the most outstanding receptionist available?'.

The three characteristics are:

- *Proactive: what can I do?*
- *Excellence: what is the highest standard I can deliver?*
- *Ownership: what can I influence? How am I a part of this?*

In summary, to develop level 2 on the career compass point:

- *Do what you love and love what you do.*
- *Ensure what you do is an essential part of your being.*
- *Raise your standards.*
- *Take ownership.*

Mind/body

As we look after our body, experience it, stretch it and nurture it, we notice whole new levels of integration. As we care for it and sleep sufficiently and meditate we notice that our creativity is soaring. This helps us to pursue our dreams via dharma. It helps us to do that which we feel more inclined towards anyway. Things which once seemed such an effort are now effortless. We are less dependent upon stimulants to keep us going. Our moods are more predictable and no longer swing wildly.

We find that we are thinking in new ways. Not in 'struggle' ways, but in possibility ways. Not 'moving away' (for example, 'I don't want to work with him') ways, but 'let's do it, let's find a way' ways.

We feel a higher force, a new development, a higher consciousness. If it is part of our belief set we feel closer to our spiritual path. If not, then we are delighted that we have accessed a part of our brain that contains potential skills such as intuition, synchronicity and so on, and that these are more available to us. We finally realize that perhaps the reason why intuition and synchronicity are so inconsistently available, so non-measurable in a scientific way, is that they are very dependent upon our state, our being. If a simple transaction with someone can go better or worse depending upon our state, then certainly such higher stuff as this will undoubtedly be benefited hugely – or not – by our state.

Again, let's examine where we were. And now let's examine where we are going:

- *At level 0, mind and body are very much separate. A headache: oh, well. Worried a bit. Oh, well. No connections are noticed and we typically fix the symptoms with a drug such as aspirin and the body will regularly show symptoms of abuse: excess stress, lack of sleep.*
- *At level 1, mind and body are connected. Of course if we worry, we are going to experience stress. We will be experiencing flow state more often, particularly as we take an integrated (MEDS) approach to our work. We 'notice' how we are feeling and act upon the feedback that we get.*

- *At level 2, mind and body are one, we are more concerned with our spirit; our health is excellent. Higher skills such as intuition and synchronicity become more regularly available to us.*

If entrepreneurial thinking is key to career, then spirit is the key to level 2 mind/body. What do I mean by spirit, again? I don't mean religion, I mean that which is integrated sufficiently to release our own potential. So how do you develop your spirituality? Here are ten guidelines:

- *Invest in yourself. Remember that you are organic and need TLC (tender loving care).*
- *Take time out. Meditate. Walk regularly.*
- *Take food and drink which builds and repairs.*
- *Take MEDS to a fully integrated model.*
- *Read inspirational material.*
- *Spend time with inspirational people.*
- *Be in inspirational places.*
- *Contribute.*
- *Think about who you are.*
- *Expect uncertainty and challenges on your spiritual path.*

Finance

At the starter level, finance seems so dull for so many. It's about details, it's about 'stuff I don't understand', as many people will complain. And yet once begun, we realize it is the practical side of the route to so much of what we want: freedom, growth, opportunity. As we give it attention we find it's not so difficult after all to develop our finances: to begin to save, to get out of debt, to even begin to invest some money. That then gives us an outstanding opportunity to realize that having all this money is not such a motivator after all! In fact, money is firstly a hygiene factor for most people, something that if missing is a demotivator, but which is not a motivator in itself. Secondly, it is useful for some toys like a car or a bigger house. Finally it is a measure, a calibration of how we are doing. After that, our real craving is for intangibles: fun, laughter. We can get those often without needing vast sums of money. And as we move from simple finance to affluence we realize true affluence is about:

- *Having the basics covered: being able to pay the rent/mortgage.*
- *Gratitude for being able to address our compass needs.*
- *Contribution: the ability to help others.*
- *Spirit: discovering who we really are.*

We truly begin to let go of the need for stuff and remind ourselves of what is truly important, that we are fortunate with basics such as good health, the roof over our head and a job. So:

- *Level 0 finance is about money, control/cost.*
- *Level 1 finance is about: affluence/money management.*
- *Level 2 finance is about abundance/flow.*

The higher level of finance is abundance. Suddenly instead of struggling it happens. Here are five ways to develop abundance:

- *Appreciate what you have.*
- *Contribute to others.*
- *Slip into a flow state.*
- *Go with that flow.*
- *Work to your talents.*

Relationships

And as we get these to work, by being attentive, appreciative and acting first, we bring true joy into our lives. Once again we realize that we do not need to seek happiness 'out there'. Happiness comes from within, once we begin to establish appropriate relationships. It is, of course, largely about reaching out, about love. Once again this brings us back to spirit. Relationships are much about communication: about spending time with a person and realizing how different they are. And that it doesn't matter. Because it just is. And you won't change it. So why not learn to appreciate it and work with it?

As our relationships blossom, although we have difficulties we realize they need not be permanent but something which simply needs a bit of attention: that, of course, brings a whole new dimension to the rest of our lives. Here are the three levels as applied to relationships:

- *Level 0: control, jealousy. This level is the level at which we believe that because we have a relationship with someone, we have a right to control them (whether it be a personal relationship or a working one). Our expectation is that the person should behave as we do or as we want them to.*
- *Level 1: love, support. At this level we understand terms such as 'karma', the 'golden rule'. With such approaches we make progress in our relationships.*
- *Level 2: abundance, freedom. Here we have such trust. In our personal relationship we know that the only way we will get true love is if we are able to love ourselves by having an appropriate level of freedom and authenticity.*

Fun

Fun is the whole point. Fun, of course, is part of all of the compass points: it's part of healthy relationships, it's part of physical development, it's part of our finances being in order. Fun is a true aspect of spirit. It has been said that a true sign of enlightenment is light-heartedness and the manifestation of desire. And now for the three levels:

- *Level 0: beer. Level 0 is the stuff level, whether that level is a game of football, several cans of beer, a stint of retail therapy.*
- *Level 1: love. This is when we realize we get the most fun by giving, by going beyond ourselves and helping others.*
- *Level 2: authenticity. We have fun because we are true to ourselves.*

What connects it all? A sense of light-heartedness.

Contribution

I'm sure you've got the hang of this now, so I'll be brief and you can elaborate if you feel the need to. So what are the three levels for contribution?

- *Level 0: nothing, or contributing begrudgingly.*
- *Level 1: making a regular effort.*
- *Level 2: abundance thinking.*

What connects it all? A sense of humility.

As each compass point develops, it is supportive of the others. As each supports the others a simplicity appears. Thus:

- *Career = authenticity.*
- *Mind/body = spirit.*
- *Finance = affluence.*
- *Relationships = love.*
- *Fun = light-heartedness.*
- *Contribution = humility.*

Chapter 13
LifeCompass: Begin

Now truly is the time to start work if you haven't before.

- *Decide your compass points.*
- *Live by your compass.*
- *Have fun.*

If you would like to do work on your compass in a workshop environment, you may well enjoy attending my programme: Personal Excellence. For more details, telephone +44 (0) 1865 301666 or send an email via www.strategicedge.co.uk.

And good luck once more!

Index